THE WORLD'S FAVORITE ROSES

A rose smiled at me from the hedge,
My heart responded happily.
And something nudged me from life's edge
As who was rose, and who was me?
Between ourselves there's little but
A subtle change of chemistry.

J. L. H.

J. L. HARKNESS

THE WORLD'S FAVORITE ROSES

AND HOW TO GROW THEM

MCGRAW-HILL BOOK COMPANY

NEW YORK   ST. LOUIS   SAN FRANCISCO

Any nose
May ravage with impunity a rose.

ROBERT BROWNING

A McGraw-Hill Co-Publication

Library of Congress Cataloging in
Publication Data
Harkness, Jack Leigh.
    The world's favorite roses and
    how to grow them.
    Bibliography: p.
    Includes index
    1. Roses. 2. Rose culture.
    I. Title.
SB411.H323   635.9'53'372
79-11530

ISBN 0-07-026470-8

Original Concept and Design by:
EMIL M. BUEHRER

Editor:
DAVID BAKER

Managing Editor:
FRANCINE PEETERS

Designer:
CHARLES WHITEHOUSE

Picture Procuration:
LILIANE FIELD
ROSARIA PASQUARIELLO

Production Manager:
FRANZ GISLER

Graphic Artist:
FRANZ CORAY

Printed in Switzerland

Printed by:
IMPRIMERIES REUNIES, LAUSANNE, SWITZERLAND
Bound by:
CH. BUSENHART, LAUSANNE, SWITZERLAND
Composition by:
FOTOSATZ FEBEL AG, BASEL, SWITZERLAND
Photolithography by:
ACTUAL, BIEL, SWITZERLAND (Color sections)
HEGO AG, LITTAU, SWITZERLAND (black & white)

CONTENTS

Descendants of the Wild Rose   6
Where our garden roses came from. The rose's place in nature. The genus Rosa, *its family tree and history. Human contributions to a long and rich development.*

A Rosarian's Portfolio of
Outstanding Roses: Portfolio I   16
Color photographs of 123 of the most beautiful and most growable roses in the world, arranged according to class. First of four color portfolios.

Description of the Roses in Portfolio I   33
Word-portraits of the roses illustrated in color: the scent, size, hardiness, habits, needs, and particular uses of each rose.

A World of Roses:
The 21 Principal Types   41
Survey of the wide variety of rose classes new and old—the Hybrid teas, Floribundas, Gallicas, Damasks, Wild Roses, and many more.

Portfolio II   49
Color photographs of the outstanding varieties, continued.

Description of the Roses in Portfolio II   65
Continuation of the detailed commentaries on each rose illustrated in color.

Enjoying Your Roses   73
Enjoyment both outside and indoors. Gardening schemes for single plants, clumps, beds, hedges, borders, climbers. Cut-flower arranging. Exhibiting. Propagating.

Portfolio III   89
Color photographs of the outstanding varieties, continued.

Description of the Roses in Portfolio III   105
Detailed commentaries on each rose illustrated in color.

The Rose Breeders   113
The science and art of rose hybridization. Success stories of the major breeders of our century in all parts of the world.

Portfolio IV   121
Color photographs of the outstanding varieties; conclusion.

Description of the Roses in Portfolio IV   137
Detailed commentaries on each rose illustrated in color.

How to Grow Roses   145
Step-by-step advice, with charts and sketches: choosing the site, preparing the soil, planting, year-round and seasonal maintenance, feeding, health care, pruning.

Appendix: Vital Statistics on
300 Additional Rose Varieties   173
A supplementary chart offering brief, detailed characterization of roses not included in the Color Portfolios.

Rose Gardens to Visit   178

National Rose Societies   179

Selected Bibliography   180

Picture Credits   180

Rose Index   181

General Index   184

DESCENDANTS OF THE WILD ROSE

The wild rose growing free in the countryside—such as Rosa filipes, *in the photograph—shows us the original flower as it existed before any of man's cultivation. All wild roses are either shrubs or climbers. and many. like this example. will climb through trees.*

The flower most admired, most loved, and most widely cultivated throughout the world today is surely the rose. For all its popularity, however, the rose remains a subject on which most people know very little.

This book seeks to emphasize a basic fact about roses that is generally overlooked: that within the genus *Rosa* there are many different kinds, many different roses, beyond the Hybrid Teas and Floribundas so popular today.

In this new work on roses, we are offering as much of this fascinating diversity, in word and picture, as is possible in the space of one book. The portfolios of brilliant color photographs interspersed throughout, like flowerbeds placed here and there in a garden, set off the chapters of information on such subjects as rose types and rose selection, gardening, arranging, planting and cultivation, and about the great breeders and discoverers of new rose varieties. In this introductory chapter, we start at the beginning, with the wild rose from which all other roses derive.

Before ever there was such a thing as a national boundary, or even a nation to mark it, or even a man and woman on the face of the earth, wild roses grew in the places we call China and Japan, across Central Asia to North Africa and Europe, and in North America. They were of many species and different appearances, living in all kinds of places: prairies, forests, mountains, in the center of a continent or by the sea. Their homelands were the temperate zones of the northern hemisphere. They did not cross the equator.

Of their first treatment at the hands of men, we know nothing. It may be that lost civilizations of the past developed roses which perished shortly after their masters. Our knowledge is squeezed out of the last two and a half thousand years, and for most of that period it is scanty and vague. Scanty, because the aged records are also scanty, and deal with great gods and kings, battles, murder, and sudden death, rather than with streams and flowers. Vague, because plants were vaguely named, until Linnaeus established an orderly system in the eighteenth century.

It seems clear that roses developed to their present beauty because the people of three separate regions of the world began to cultivate and improve their native wild roses. These regions are all in Asia: in China; in the center, around Iran; and westward from Iran to the Middle East.

The oldest records do not report the earliest work. They are from Greece, and they tell of roses already being grown for their beauty and fragrance, particularly for the purpose of making rose-scented oil. The assumption is that ancient Greeks inherited their roses from older civilizations in Asia Minor and Crete. In fact, one of the first Greek references is the famous quotation from the poetess Sappho, who gave the rose the title it has held ever since, "Queen of Flowers." Quite clearly the rose had developed considerably by her time, about 600 B.C. What kind of roses did she know? It is assumed that they had been developed from a species native to those areas, *R. gallica,* known for centuries as the Red Rose.

About 150 years later, the historian Herodotus mentioned roses in the Gardens of Midas, "with sixty petals, smelling sweeter than any in the world."

A treatise, *Enquiry into Plants,* was written by Theophrastus about 300 B.C. He explained the importance of pruning, and quoted contemporary accounts of roses with a hundred petals. Roses appeared on various coins, of which some from Rhodes (named for its roses) are still preserved.

The Romans took over all they wanted from the Greeks, and made much of their roses. They even imported cut roses

Crimson 'Anne of Geierstein' a hybrid of the Eglanteria or Sweet Briar rose. retains many characteristics of its wild parent.

Center: *The wild Sweet Briar. Rosa eglanteria (or Rosa rubiginosa). noted for its long arching shoots. short flowering season. and marvelous fragrance. Out of such humble flowers have come the glorious roses of our gardens and flower shops today.*

from North Africa, to provide blooms before Roman roses were in flower. The Roman growers learned to force their flowers into earlier bloom by using hot water, to the detriment of the North African growers.

After the fall of Rome the Dark Ages fell upon Europe; and the survival of roses was due largely to the monasteries of Christendom. No longer were roses grown to subscribe to the luxuries and extravagances of ancient Rome. Their main purpose was now for medicine. Various preparations were made to cure all sorts of troubles, from toothache to piles; and rose water was taken as a tonic, which may seem fairly reasonable, for the hips contain vitamin C—in those days citrus fruit was not a universal source of that ingredient.

By the year 1700, the roses of Europe were of three main kinds, of which the salient features were white, pink, or red colors; fragrance; and blooms in summer only. They were the Gallicas, which possibly came from the days of antiquity; the Damasks, which were like pale-colored Gallicas, of more open and arching growth; and the Albas, dense shrubs with a suggestion of Dog Rose about them. In addition to these, the Centifolias were then being developed; and there were a few foreign imports, especially the Musk Rose, and a yellow rose from farther east. Which is a reminder that the people of China and of Central Asia had also been interested in roses.

The small engravings of old roses on these pages come from a German herbal printed in 1713 (and are labeled with their contemporary names).

Below: Rosa milesia flora simpl. *and* Rosa provincialia flora alba.

THE CHINA ROSES

Of all the countries in the world, China was the most richly endowed by nature in the number and the beauty of its different wild roses. That country is also notable for the fact that whereas in most of the world civilizations have flourished and then disappeared, as if their denizens were indeed a species both distinct and extinct, China appears on the surface to have maintained a more settled continuity of life.

No records tell what the Chinese did with their wild roses, nor when they did it; it may well have been a thousand years before Europeans discovered those amazing achievements. Chinese roses came to Europe from about 1750, not by hazardous explorations into the interior, but by the simple process of calling upon the Fa Tee Nursery, on the south bank of the Pearl River outside the walled city of Canton. Canton is now Kwangchow; its wall disappeared years ago to be replaced by a road, the city was modernized by the Chi-

Above: Rosa rubra praecox flor. simplici.; Rosa spinosa *(with many thorns); and* Rosa cinnamomea.

Right: *Woodcut of* Rosa lutea, *from a 1687 herbal.*

Below: Rosa flore alba plena *and* Rosa milesia flor. rubro pleno.

Far right: Rosa silv. flore rub.; Rosa centifolia rubra *(the name indicating that it has one hundred petals, unlike the wild roses); and* Rosa alba flora simplic.

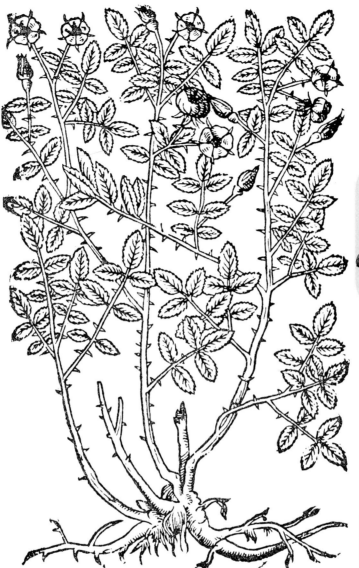

nese, knocked down by the Japanese, and built again. But to rosarians it is a hallowed place, where old sailing ships called, and brought back roses destined to change the gardens of the whole world.

These Chinese roses differed from European roses in several respects, the most important of which was their habit of flowering on every shoot they made. European roses were finished after one burst into bloom in the summer; any shoots which grew thereafter had no flower buds. Their flowers would have to wait for the following summer, when they would appear on side shoots.

But the Chinese roses went on growing into winter, and every shoot had a flower at its apex, month after month.

One of them in fact became known as the Monthly Rose from the regularity of its performance. It is still grown, under the names 'Old Blush' or 'Common Blush China.' It came into Europe from Canton in 1752.

The Chinese roses had smooth and glossy foliage with pretty colors in it; a contrast to the dull green leaves of Europe. The Chinese had a quality of iridiscence about their petals, and a delicate scent. They were known for many years as "tea-scented China roses"; and that is the origin of the class name Hybrid Tea, borne by the most popular roses of today.

In a short time China roses were distributed about the world and began to breed with European roses. The first steps appear to have been by chance, and in extraordinarily scattered places. Of the various classes which led step by step to our modern roses, the Portlands began in Italy; the Noisettes in Charleston, South Carolina; the Bourbons in the Island of Réunion in the Indian Ocean. Thus the nations were joining with the ancients of East and West, in making the Queen of Flowers more lovely yet.

By the early nineteenth century, so many different kinds of roses had caught the remontant habit of the China roses, of flowering again and again, that they were lumped together as a class of "Perpetuals," despite their great variations. A strain developed in France upon the general mixture of Perpetual and Bourbon and Tea, and it became known as the Hybrid Perpetual class. These roses had flowers of such magnificence as to advance the popularity of the rose as never before. Soon the influence of Teas—and their unique marriage of Oriental grace and European lustiness—was strengthened still further, and by the end of the nineteenth century, the class of Hybrid Teas was firmly established, due first to French, and then British breeders.

THE SEARCH FOR THE YELLOW ROSE

Hybrid Teas would clearly be the roses of the future, except that one important color was lacking: yellow. To find it, the rosarian has to recall the third group of grand originators: the people of Central Asia, in and around Iran.

As with the Chinese, so in this case also the origins are obscure. A list of plants was compiled in the thirteenth century by Ibn-el-Awam, an Arabian expert of that time; he included a yellow rose, of which this is believed to be the earliest record.

Probably the oldest garden roses cultivated in the west are the Gallicas. The striped Rosa gallica versicolor *syn 'Rosa Mundi' dates back to 1650. Gallicas, Damasks, and Albas were the three principal rose types in Europe up to the seventeenth and eighteenth centuries.*

Centifolias, of unknown parentage, were first developed around 1550. The photograph shows the blush 'Fantin Latour.'

Below: *The apple-scented* Rosa setipoda, *one of the loveliest of wild roses, a Cinnamomea from western China.*

Probably he referred to *R. foetida,* known in our day as 'Austrian Yellow'; this is a rose of five petals, usually considered to be a wild rose, scattered about the region from Turkey to Afghanistan. The reason it bears the name of Austria is because that country was the staging post upon its journey further west. But it is a very strange wild rose, particularly in its limited fertility, which is so low as to leave room for a little suspicion as to whether it was originally a hybrid.

About 1600 there was an international exhibition in Vienna, in which a display from Turkey depicted some *double* yellow roses. No such thing had been heard of in the west; a botanist named Clusius ascertained that they truly existed, and he obtained some from Turkey. They proved to be what is known as *R. X hemisphaerica;* to our forefathers it was the Sulfur Rose.

For more than two hundred years, the Sulfur Rose was the only double yellow known to western rosarians. Then, in 1837, a far more brilliant yellow rose was introduced under the name 'Persian Yellow.' It had been obtained from Iran by a British diplomat, Sir Henry Willock. Nobody knows how long it had been growing in Iran beforehand.

'Persian Yellow' was the key to modern yellow roses, and the man to turn it in the lock was a French breeder, Joseph Pernet-Ducher. He had an amazing benefit from good luck on the way. He raised seedlings from a red Hybrid Perpetual, which had been fertilized by the pollen of 'Persian Yellow.' The seedlings were not remontant, and therefore of little apparent commercial use; but he kept them, and upon receiving a visit from a friend two or three years later, he went to show his guest the seedlings from so interesting a cross. It would appear that one of them had itself borne seed, and a seed had fallen to the ground and germinated; the two men looking at it saw the first of the yellow Hybrid Teas. It was in fact yellow and red; it was named 'Soleil d'Or' and introduced in 1900. That was the origin of the yellow roses destined to adorn the gardens of the twentieth century.

A nineteenth-century bush rose developed from R. sempervirens, 'Little White Pet' has charming double blossoms that will enliven any garden today.

'Cécile Brunner syn The Sweetheart Rose,' an outstanding hybrid developed in 1881 from China roses. The Chinas, which reached the west around 1750, offered important characteristics, including remontancy (repeated flowering within the same season).

THE GENUS 'ROSA' AND ITS MANY SPECIES

Our historical sketch has endeavored to give some idea of the vast changes that have occurred in the development from wild roses to the many varieties so admired and enjoyed today. Of course, this is a partial history at best, full of mysteries that we shall probably never fathom. But we can also

approach the mystifying diversity of the roses from a different direction: on the basis of evidence found all around us, it is possible to explore the place of this flower in nature and to survey its principal categories and subdivisions.

When botanists talk of families, they refer to a group of plants which have in common a fairly wide range of characteristics. The rose family, properly called the *Rosaceae*, includes besides roses such fruits as apples, pears, peaches, and plums. It contains about ninety sorts of plants, which have certain features in common, by which they differ from all the rest of nature.

Each of these ninety sorts is called a genus, a word implying that it was generated as a separate entity. The plural is genera. To discover a genus, the comparisons have been made on a finer scale than those which established families. The rose is a genus, one of the ninety in the rose family, and it has the Latin name *Rosa.*

Botanists, to whom the rose has always been one of the most perplexing plants, are not certain how many different species of the rose exist. They roughly define a species as a plant which comes true from its own seed. And the puzzling element about roses is that they are very capricious in this respect, and thus defy the normal criterion. The usual estimate is that there are from 120 to 150 different species.

The species may show changes from their normal character. When such changes are regularly reproduced, they are called varieties.

The species often breed between one another and produce plants to some degree different from themselves. These are hybrid species, or just hybrids.

Mankind hastens the operations of nature, and produces roses for his own purposes. There are cultivated varieties, abbreviated to "cultivars."

But in the case of roses, mankind has been at work so long, and nature so thoroughly, that often we cannot say for sure which are varieties, or hybrids, or cultivars. The word "variety" is therefore applied to all three in common usage, accepting the inherent inaccuracies; technically, it is not strictly correct. As to the number of varieties, they are as good as infinite.

Within the genus *Rosa*, comparisons can be made to separate the species into groups. This gives rise to some interesting speculations as to the origin and evolution of the rose. The chart on pages 14–15 illustrates the methods, and some of the results. The botanical terms are explained on the diagrams of the parts of the rose, opposite.

Hybrid Teas—crossbred from the tender Teas and the hardy Hybrid Perpetuals, beginning in 1867—are without doubt the most popular of roses today.

THE PARTS OF THE FLOWER

1. Pistils, the female organs, with three parts:
(a) Stigma, at top, to catch pollen.
(b) Style, the stem down which the pollen goes.

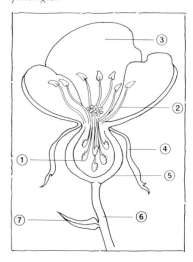

(c) Ovule, at base, to become a seed after fertilization.

2. Stamens, the male organs, with two parts:
(a) Anther, where pollen is borne.
(b) Filament, the supporting stem.

3. Petal; the petals together form the corolla.

4. Sepals; there are five. Before unfolding, they protect the bud, and are known at that stage as the calyx.

5. Ovary; it contains the embryo seeds; when ripe, it is the hip.

6. The flower stalk, or pedicil.

7. Bract (underdeveloped leaf).

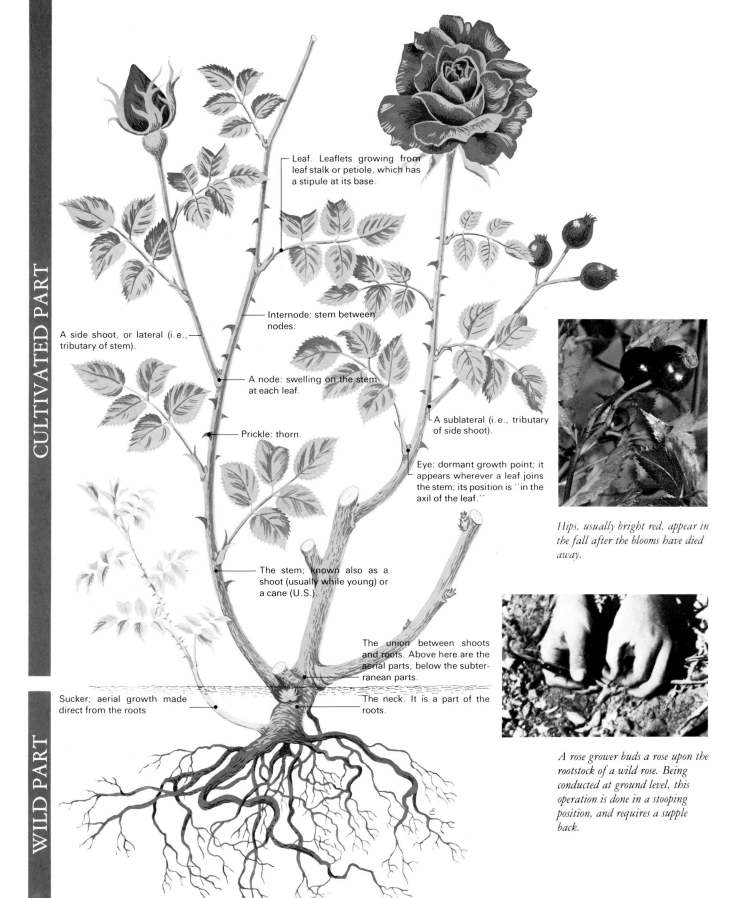

Leaf. Leaflets growing from leaf stalk or petiole, which has a stipule at its base.

Internode: stem between nodes.

A side shoot, or lateral (i.e., tributary of stem).

A node: swelling on the stem at each leaf.

Prickle: thorn.

A sublateral (i.e., tributary of side shoot).

Eye: dormant growth point; it appears wherever a leaf joins the stem; its position is "in the axil of the leaf."

The stem; known also as a shoot (usually while young) or a cane (U.S.).

The union between shoots and roots. Above here are the aerial parts, below the subterranean parts.

Sucker; aerial growth made direct from the roots

The neck. It is a part of the roots.

Hips, usually bright red, appear in the fall after the blooms have died away.

A rose grower buds a rose upon the rootstock of a wild rose. Being conducted at ground level, this operation is done in a stooping position, and requires a supple back.

THE GENUS 'ROSA'

Subgenus SIMPLICIFOLIAE
(= Simple leaves)

Disobeys the rules by having the wrong kind of leaves; they are simple, that is, just one leaf, not divided into leaflets. It has no stipules either, and botanically is not a rose, although it was for long considered one. There is only one species, *Hulthemia persica*, a plant of semi-desert regions. Its unique quality is a bright red eye in the center of the flower, which is otherwise yellow. It may be the most primitive form of the rose to have survived. From Iran and neighboring countries.

1. BANKSIANAE
(= Lady Banks' roses)

Distinguished by the stipules, not properly joined to the leaf stalk; narrow and pointed, they soon fall off. The flowers are small, carried in rounded heads. The two species are Chinese climbers; one gave us 'Banksian Yellow' *(R. banksiae lutea)*. Interesting features are the pretty form of the double sorts, similar to double primroses; the leaves, glossy on the underside; and the stems, often thornless for considerable lengths.

2. LAEVIGATAE
(= Brightly polished roses)

The stipules are similar to those in section 1, but more toothed; the flowers are large, and not in rounded heads, but often solitary. The only species is *R. laevigata* from China. The highly polished leaves are attractive.

3. BRACTEATAE
(= Roses with bracts)

The stipules are as for sections 1 and 2, but are deeply toothed. The flowers are remarkable for their bracts, which are leafy growths overlapping one another upon the seed pod in a unique style, like tiles. There is only one species, from China, interesting because its leaves do not easily fall and have more rounded ends than most rose leaves. It is also capable of rooting itself when its long shoots bend down to the ground.

4. INDICAE
(= Indian rose)

In this and all succeeding sections, the stipules are properly joined to the leaf stalks. The distinguishing feature here is the habit of the styles, which stick well out of their tube, but are separate from one another. There are only two species, one from China and the other from Burma/China; and the name was given in error, because people thought they had come from India. From the Indicae came qualities of remontancy, characteristic Tea scent, attractive leaves, and large petals. These qualities were developed by way of the China roses, Noisettes, and Teas, thus leading to our modern roses.

5. SYNSTYLAE
(= Styles together)

Distinguished from the Indicae by the styles, which protrude from their tube, and are fused together in a narrow column. About 24 species, of which 20 come from eastern Asia (mostly China), 2 from Europe, 1 from Turkey, and 1 from USA. Here we find the tree-climbing roses, which diffuse scent from stamens as well as petals. Remarkable leaves, either for being red when young *(R. filipes)*, or for glittering *(R. wichuraiana)*, or for staying in winter *(R. sempervirens)*, or for enormous size *(R. sinowilsonii)*. A valuable feature, bred into modern roses, is closely set heads formed of a multitude of blooms. From the Synstylae, with the help of other sections, have come Polyanthas, and many climbers and trailers such as 'Paul's Scarlet Climber,' 'Félicité et Perpétue,' 'American Pillar,' 'Albéric Barbier.'

Subgenus HESPERRHODOS
(= Western roses)

Distinguished by prickly hips, which remain on the plants to a late stage. There are two species, both having a fairly restricted habitat in the south to southwest of the United States. Interesting features are very sharp thorns, more like those of a gooseberry, and tiny hairs, which show up on the ends of young shoots almost like white fur. These may also be primitive roses.

Subgenus PLATYRHODON
(= The rose that flakes)

Distinguished by hips, which fall while still green. There is only one species, *R. roxburghii,* from China. It is unique in shedding its bark from its old stems. The leaves are remarkable, being composed of up to 19 leaflets.

Subgenus EUROSA
(= Real roses)

Distinguished by smooth hips, which may have bristles or hairs on them, but do not have real prickles like the other three subgenera. Nearly all roses belong to the Eurosa, which is consequently divided into the following ten sections.

6. GALLICANAE
(= French rose)

In this and all succeeding sections, the styles do not stick out from their tube noticeably. The Gallicanae, of which there is only one species, are distinguished by having flowers borne alone, or a few together, rather than in large heads. They have five leaflets. The only species, *R. gallica,* comes from Europe and West Asia, and is famous as the foundation upon which the old roses of the West were raised. It is notable among wild roses for having large flowers, good fragrance, and medicinal uses. From it, with the help of other sections, came the Gallicas, Damasks, Centifolias, Moss roses, Portlands, Bourbons, and Hybrid Perpetuals.

7. PIMPINELLIFOLIAE
(= Fine, ferny leaves like burnets)

Distinguished from the Gallicanae by normally having more than 5 leaflets. There are about 12 species, 7 from China or East Asia, 4 from central Asia, and 1 spread all the way from Siberia to Spain. That wanderer is the Scotch Rose. Valuable gifts held in this section are yellow colors *(R. ecae, R. foetida,* etc.), hardiness *(R. spinosissima),* black hips, dainty leaves, and huge red thorns *(R. sericea pteracantha).* This section contributed to modern yellow roses, produced some beautiful hybrids such as 'Canary Bird' and 'Golden Chersonese,' and gave rise to the Scotch roses.

8. CANINAE
(= Dog roses)

In sections 8, 9, 10, the flowers are borne in large heads of many blooms. The Caninae are distinguished by curved thorns. About 30 species, the majority European. Its unique sexual process matches 7 male chromosomes to 28 female; it provides Vitamin C, a great many rootstocks, besides such features as the red-purple leaves of *Rosa rubrifolia.* It gave us the handsome Albas.

9. CAROLINAE
(= Roses from Carolina)

Distinguished from the Caninae by straight thorns. The sepals usually fall before the hips are ripe. Seven species, all from North America, the only roses which grow in wet ground and in shade. Beautiful leaves assume lovely autumnal colors.

10. CINNAMOMEAE
(= Cinnamon roses)

Distinguished from the Carolinae by the sepals remaining attached to the ripened hips. About 56 species, with much diversity; China and USA have 21 each, 13 are from Asia, 1 from Europe. The section includes 2 roses with whitened leaves; the most beautiful hips in the genus; dainty leaves; an almost thornless rose *(Rosa pendulina,* the sole European); the healthiest rose, with leaves difficult for blackspot to enter *(R. rugosa).* Hybrids have been raised more from *R. rugosa* than any other.

A ROSARIAN'S PORTFOLIO OF OUTSTANDING ROSES

The author's selection of 123 important rose varieties are illustrated in color in the portfolios that begin on pages 17, 49, 89, 121, and these roses are thoroughly described in the texts that follow the color sections. The alphabetical list below gives the illustration number for each of these 123 roses; the same number refers the reader to the description text for a particular rose.

89	ALBÉRIC BARBIER	13	GRANDPA DICKSON	101	ROSA ECAE
5	ALEC'S RED	82	HANDEL	98	ROSA FARRERI PERSETOSA
2	ALEXANDER	57	ICEBERG		
39	ALLGOLD	15	JOHN WATERER	100	ROSA FOETIDA
75	ALTISSIMO	17	JOSEPHINE BRUCE	104	ROSA FOETIDA BICOLOR
42	ANNE COCKER	14	JUST JOEY	90	ROSA GALLICA VERSICOLOR
41	ANNE HARKNESS	16	KORDES' PERFECTA		
43	ARTHUR BELL	51	KORRESIA	116	ROSA RUBRIFOLIA
104	AUSTRIAN COPPER	114	LADY PENZANCE	121	ROSA RUGOSA ALBA
100	AUSTRIAN YELLOW	91	LEVERKUSEN	113	ROSA SERICEA PTERACANTHA
80	BABY FAURAX	50	LILLI MARLENE		
63	BABY MASQUERADE	73	MME GRÉGOIRE STAECHELIN	103	ROSA SPINOSISSIMA HISPIDA
86	BALLERINA				
76	BANTRY BAY	93	MME HARDY	117	ROSA VIRGINIANA
9	BLESSINGS	95	MME PIERRE OGER	119	ROSA X PRUHONICIANA
20	BLUE MOON	107	MAIGOLD	32	ROSE GAUJARD
62	BUFF BEAUTY	49	MARGARET MERRIL	123	ROSERAIE DE L'HAŸ
112	CANARY BIRD	106	MARGUERITE HILLING	68	ROSINA
4	CÉCILE BRUNNER	48	MARLENA	72	ROYAL GOLD
111	CELESTIAL	87	MAY QUEEN	56	SAGA
46	CIRCUS	3	MERMAID	60	SARABANDE
97	CHAPEAU DE NAPOLÉON	21	MICHÈLE MEILLAND	122	SCABROSA
6	CHICAGO PEACE	19	MISCHIEF	36	SILVER JUBILEE
64	CINDERELLA	23	MOJAVE	33	SONIA MEILLAND
71	COMPASSION	85	MOZART	61	SOUTHAMPTON
110	COMPLICATA	24	NATIONAL TRUST	96	SOUVENIR DE LA MALMAISON
66	CORNELIA	109	NEVADA		
77	DANSE DU FEU	88	NEW DAWN	108	STANWELL PERPETUAL
8	DIORAMA	67	NEW PENNY	59	STARGAZER
10	ELIZABETH HARKNESS	22	OPHELIA	70	STARINA
74	ENA HARKNESS	25	PASCALI	18	SUNBLEST
45	ESCAPADE	26	PEACE	51	SUNSPRITE
44	EUROPEANA	29	PEEP O' DAY	35	SUPER STAR
84	FÉLICITÉ ET PERPÉTUE	65	PENELOPE	34	SUTTER'S GOLD
12	FIRST LOVE	28	PICCADILLY	69	SWEET FAIRY
11	FRAGRANT CLOUD	27	PINK FAVORITE	4	SWEETHEART ROSE
118	FRAU DAGMAR HARTOPP	53	PINK PARFAIT	33	SWEET PROMISE
47	FRENSHAM	79	PINK PERPETUE	92	THE FAIRY
51	FRIESIA	81	POMPON DE PARIS	35	TROPICANA
115	FRITZ NOBIS	31	PRECIOUS PLATINUM	40	TYPHOON
102	FRÜHLINGSGOLD	55	PRINCESS CHICHIBU	38	VIOLINISTA COSTA
120	GERANIUM	52	PROMINENT	37	WENDY CUSSONS
99	GOLDEN CHERSONESE	54	QUEEN ELIZABETH	83	YESTERDAY
78	GOLDEN SHOWERS	30	RED DEVIL	94	ZÉPHIRINE DROUHIN
7	GOLDEN WAVE	58	ROB ROY		
105	GOLDEN WINGS	1	ROSA BANKSIAE LUTEA		

1

Rosa Banksiae Lutea

2 Alexander

3 Mermaid

18

4   Cécile Brunner

5   Alec's Red

19

7   Dr. A. J. Verhage

Blessings   9

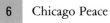

6   Chicago Peace

8   Diorama

10 Elizabeth Harkness 11 Duftwolke

13 Grandpa Dickson

Just Joey 14

John Waterer 15

17 Josephine Bruce

Kordes' Perfecta 16

Landora

Mischief

21   Michèle Meilland

20   Mainzer Fastnacht

23 Mojave

Pascali 25

24 National Trust

22 Ophelia

26 Mme A. Meilland
(Peace)

Pink Favorite 27

28   Piccadilly

29   Peep o' Day

Red Devil 30

Precious Platinum 31

1

R. BANKSIAE LUTEA
syn YELLOW BANKSIAN

Banksianae

A vigorous climber, which produces bunches of charming yellow flowers, like round posies made out of double yellow prim-roses, uniquely lovely. It can be grown on the wall of a house or over a small building or trellis.
'Yellow Banksian' can grow into a huge plant in a favorable climate, but can be killed by exposure to subzero temperatures, especially if not sheltered from biting winds. It flowers only once in the year, very early at that. It makes a main shoot one year, side shoots from it in year two, and subsidiary side shoots in year three; then it flowers from those subsidiaries, which must not therefore be pruned off.
It was raised in China, when and by whom we do not know; the original form was the wild single white *R. banksiae normalis.* This yellow variety was brought to England by John Banks in 1824.
It can easily be propagated from cuttings.

2

ALEXANDER
syn ALEXANDRA

Hybrid Tea

Color is 'Alexander's' trump card, especially when the sun strikes the luminous orange vermilion petals and shows a red rose trying to outdo the orange nasturtium. No other rose is the same. The growth is tall, with gleaming dark leaves, and long stems. The flowers are not full, having 22 large petals, frequently scalloped. The buds and young flowers are elegant, with pointed centers. The old flowers open wide and clean, to show their stamens. It is a fine rose in the garden, good to cut; it can make an excellent hedge, about shoulder high, flowers and leaves gleaming.
Raised in England by the author from 'Super Star' × Seedling, it was introduced in 1972. It is highly esteemed in Britain, Germany, Switzerland, France, Australia, and New Zealand; and although not yet widely grown in the United States, it is in the American Rose Society's *Buying Guide.*

3

MERMAID

Hybrid Bracteata

One of the most free-flowering climbers; it is supremely beautiful, having large creamy flowers of only five petals with a mass of amber stamens, which force the eye to take them as the focal point, the governors of color and size. This vision of delicacy may by enjoyed for about four months or so each year. It is a strong grower, conveniently managed on a house wall.
'Mermaid' can perish in consequence of a severe frosty winter. It has brittle stems, which are likely to snap out when being tied in; and it should be daintily pruned, by merely tipping young growth, and cutting out only that which is dead or damaged. It was raised in England from *R. bracteata* × a Tea rose by Arthur Paul and introduced in 1918.
R. bracteata is a wild Chinese rose.
It is said to be resistant to blackspot, and indeed 'Mermaid' rarely suffers from that disease.

4

CÉCILE BRUNNER
syn SWEETHEART ROSE

Hybrid China

This Hybrid China rose is adored for its pretty little buds, which although of perfect rose shape are only about fingernail size. They are quite irresistible; and if pinned to a lady's dress give the same charm to her. The color is light pink.

This rose may be had as a bush, in which case it is remontant; or as a climber, in which case it flowers chiefly in summer, with a few later flowers. There is also a vigorous remontant shrub with similar flowers, rather coarser in appearance, called 'Bloomfield Abundance.' Our photograph shows the climber. The original 'Cécile Brunner' was raised by the widow Ducher in France and introduced in 1881. It was to be expected that improvements on the same lines would have swiftly followed, for its character is simple, and its color unremarkable. But it has never been surpassed in the beauty and neatness of its buds.

5

ALEC'S RED

Hybrid Tea

Its best point is fragrance, for it has a sweet and strong smell, very delicious. Next we admire its size and form. The buds are wide at the base, shaped like tulip bulbs. Each expands into a fat flower of about 45 petals, the outer petals spreading wide, while the inner form a handsome, pointed center. From that point it falls from grace, and finishes with the center congested, confused, and low. The light crimson color may prove disappointing if we hoped for a dark red rose; but it has the virtue of holding reasonably true. 'Alec's Red' was raised in Scotland by Alexander Cocker, from 'Duftwolke' × 'Dame de Coeur.' It was introduced in 1970 and has had particularly good reports from Britain, Germany, the United States, and Western Australia. It made Mr. Cocker's name as a formidable rose breeder, in only his second year of introducing the varieties he had raised.

6

CHICAGO PEACE

Hybrid Tea

Some people prefer this rose to the famous 'Peace,' of which it is almost a twin. 'Chicago Peace' differs only in its color, which is a lively phlox pink, based and backed with yellow. It forms a fine, large bloom of about 40 petals. The growth is tall and bushy, but not usually quite as big as that of 'Peace.'

It is a sport, that is to say, a natural mutation of 'Peace,' and as such, it will occasionally revert to the yellow of its progenitor. An excellent garden rose, and very good for cutting. 'Chicago Peace' was noticed among his plants of 'Peace' by Stanley C. Johnston of Wheaton, Illinois. The Conard-Pyle Company introduced it in 1962. It is rated excellent in the United States, and highly in nearly every country where roses are grown.

Now that the color of 'Peace' is no longer as exciting as when first seen, people turn instead to 'Chicago Peace.'

7

DR. A. J. VERHAGE
syn GOLDEN WAVE

Hybrid Tea

In color, form, and perfume, this rose is impeccable. The lovely color is golden yellow with a slight apricot flush; the flowers are large, formed of about 25 petals, with a firm center, elegant to a point; the scent is strong.

Unfortunately the growth is rather squat and apt to suffer from frost, so that one is obliged to warn those in colder countries against this lovely rose unless they can grow it under glass, where it is particularly fine.

It was raised by Gijsbert Verbeek in Holland from 'Tawny Gold' × Seedling. Verbeek was interested in breeding florist's roses, rather than garden roses; he introduced it in 1960; and the Carlton Rose Nurseries, Carlton, Oregon, brought it out under its synonym in the United States in 1963. A favorite rose for its beauty, it is recommended highly in South Africa, South Australia, and other lands.

8

DIORAMA

Hybrid Tea

A fine yellow rose, with much warmth in the color, for it is no plain yellow, but has the smallest touch of amber to enliven it. The outer petals are heavily flushed red; and often (too often, some might say) the red spreads further into the bloom. The 27 petals are large and substantial, forming a handsome bloom. The scent is pleasant, but not generously supplied.

The bushes grow with agreeable vigor and flower freely, being especially good late in the season; for although 'Diorama' is a good summer rose, it is an outstanding fall one.

It was raised by de Ruiter of Hazerswoude, Holland, from 'Peace' × 'Beauté,' and introduced in 1965. Although 'Peace' mothered the seed, 'Diorama' does not show much affinity to that famous rose. The leaves and color derive more from 'Beauté'; 'Peace' lent some of its vigor, because 'Beauté' is not a strong grower.

9

BLESSINGS

Hybrid Tea

Pink and plentiful, 'Blessings' ranks among the finest bedding roses. It provides a mass of pink flowers, which will hold together almost as evenly as the surface of a lake. The blooms are on the small side for a Hybrid Tea, moderately fragrant, with about 30 petals, of neat and pleasing shape. The color, a bright rose pink, not deep, holds well. 'Blessings' is a workmanlike, functional rose, rather than an exotic beauty. Walter Gregory raised 'Blessings' in England from 'Queen Elizabeth' × an unknown variety and introduced the rose in 1968. It is grown over most of Europe and in North America, and less often in the warmer countries.

This may be because its flowers open more quickly in the sun; but possibly it is not known as it should be. So efficient a flower producer ought not to be passed by without the trial it deserves.

10

ELIZABETH HARKNESS

Hybrid Tea

Wide, pale flowers exhibit charming subtleties of form and color. The outer petals stretch out to a great span, leaving a charming heart, low and slightly open. The ivory color may tend at times to blush or buff, and the tips of the central petals occasionally assume a charming rosy-pink tint. Usually there are about 34 petals; they issue a sweet scent.

Like many pale roses, 'Elizabeth Harkness' can only stand a limited amount of rain, and it is certainly a far better rose in summer weather. The growth is bushy, spreading out well. Raised in England by the author from 'Red Dandy' × 'Piccadilly' and introduced in 1969, it is generally rated fair, those who particularly like pale-colored roses being in an adoring minority.

One of the features of this rose is the regularity with which nearly every flower attains perfection in form and size, weather of course permitting.

11

DUFTWOLKE
syn FRAGRANT CLOUD

Hybrid Tea

'Duftwolke,' 'Fragrant Cloud'—the names point out the great attraction of this rose: its rich, penetrating scent. A cloud is left over the color, most fittingly, for after the first flush of youth, the flowers swiftly lose their bright geranium red and are turned over to dullness. They have about 31 petals and tend to be rather smaller than one would expect, owing to their liking to appear several together on one stem.

The plants are bushy, not tall; they bloom freely. The leaves are dark, fairly glossy, and not altogether successful in resisting blackspot.

Whatever shortcomings have been pointed out, they melted away under the influence of perfume, for 'Duftwolke' has become one of the most popular roses in the whole world since its introduction in 1963. It was raised by Mathias Tantau in Germany from Seedling × 'Prima Ballerina.'

12

FIRST LOVE

Hybrid Tea

Delicate grace of form distinguishes this rose, so beautifully and appropriately named. The buds are slim, carried on stems so thornless that a bunch can usually be squeezed without pain. The flowers open to a clear rose pink, with attractive points to the petals. There are about 22 petals.

The blooms are fairly small for a Hybrid Tea and have little scent. The plants grow in rather a dainty way, slim and upright. 'First Love' is translated to 'Premier Amour' in France; it was raised in California by Herbert Swim from 'Charlotte Armstrong' × 'Show Girl,' and introduced by Armstrong Nurseries in 1951. It is rated good in the United States; is a general favorite over most of Australia and New Zealand; and although the pressure of more vigorous new introductions is pushing it out of European catalogues, it is treasured by its owners.

13

GRANDPA DICKSON
syn IRISH GOLD

Hybrid Tea

Perfection in size and form of bloom—is that the consummation of the Hybrid Tea class? If so, a well-grown 'Grandpa Dickson' can attain it. The long petals, about 33 of them, are molded and sculpted like protective shells about a cone of purity. The color helps too, a cool yellow, verging toward lime.

On the debit side is its behavior in hot, dry weather, when the flowers are smaller and quickly flushed with red. In such conditions, this rose needs shade, and probably water. This plant has to be *grown*, not left to itself, if its potential is to be seen.

It was raised by Patrick Dickson in Northern Ireland, and introduced in 1966. The parents were Seedling × 'Piccadilly.' It is rated good in the United States, Britain, and New Zealand and is considered one of the best roses in most countries, especially by exhibitors.

It has often proved to be 'Queen of the Show.'

14

JUST JOEY

Hybrid Tea

A unique and beautiful color, coppery red going pale at the edges, so attractive as to stand out in any company. The flowers are large and well formed to a pointed center, having about 32 petals; and they open wide and beautiful at the end of their career. Sometimes the petals are scalloped; and there is not much scent. The bushes are of moderate vigor, rather below average height.

'Just Joey' was raised from 'Duftwolke' × 'Dr. A. J. Verhage' by Roger Pawsey of Cants, in England. It was introduced in 1973. One of the more popular new roses in Britain, it is finding its way in other countries, particularly in Holland.

It shows that most valuable attribute of a new rose, *novelty*. One would have thought it an indispensable factor, but some new roses make one wonder how they are supposed to differ from the older. No other is like 'Just Joey.'

15

JOHN WATERER

Hybrid Tea

It is dark red and holds its flowers upright; and there you have its best qualities, which are in fact rare among roses. The form is good, and the flowers substantial, for they have about 40 petals. The bushes are strong, sturdily upright, taller than average.

As the flowers open, they keep their handsome form and show darker marks on the petals, as if inclined to burn. Fortunately they escape the possible consequences of that habit; but by no means are they able to acquire that gift which all red roses should have, but which 'John Waterer' lacks: fragrance.

Raised by Sam McGredy in Northern Ireland from 'King of Hearts' × 'Hanne,' this rose was introduced in 1970. It is rated good in the United States; after a good reception in Britain, it is slowly improving its status in many countries.

This it particularly deserves for its health.

16

KORDES' PERFECTA

Hybrid Tea

A rose for the admirer of a large and stately bloom, which grows from as ugly a bud as one might expect to find. Once grown, the flower is creamy white, with rose red speckled and flushed in the petals, and marking their tips. There are about 65 petals, sufficient to make a large bloom, slow to open and magnificent.

Although the bush grows and flowers well, it is not a great ornament in the garden; 'Kordes' Perfecta' looks best in a vase; it has only slight scent.

Raised in Germany by Wilhelm Kordes from 'Golden Scepter' × 'Karl Herbst' and introduced in 1957, this rose was speedily grown all round the world; it is still an international favorite for exhibitors.

The gardener who owns a glasshouse can grow this rose to perfection, either in a pot, or planted in the soil. The result may well be the finest blooms he ever saw.

17

JOSEPHINE BRUCE

Hybrid Tea

This rose exists because it is the darkest red, the nearest to black of all. Early in the season, the flowers are often superb and shapely, with about 24 petals, all with a velvet pile. Later, they will most likely be scalloped, misshapen, and surrounded by mildewy leaves. They occasionally open their petals right out, to show yellow stamens. The bushes are rather short and spreading. 'Josephine Bruce' was raised in England by Bees Ltd. from 'Crimson Glory' × 'Madge Whipp.' The date of introduction is vague, and varies from 1949 to 1952 or 1953. In the march of progress, the experts are passing poor Josephine by, but the ordinary people have not forgotten her.

Sometimes, as in our photograph, a more scarlet color appears, but with the same velvet pile, as we trust the picture reveals. In the early summer 'Josephine Bruce' can be a useful exhibition rose.

18

LANDORA syn SUNBLEST

Hybrid Tea

An upright growing bush, obediently holding up pleasant yellow flowers on straight stems. The buds are elegant, the flowers not very large, having about 30 petals. They are good for cutting.

It is the scarcity of pure yellow varieties which earns this quite ordinary rose a place in the limelight. Yellows are either heavily flushed red or pink, or else they err from the desired growth pattern. Here is one reasonable in both respects: it is yellow and well behaved. It comes from Germany, where Mathias Tantau raised it from Seedling × 'King's Ransom' and introduced it in 1970. It is internationally commended, not so much out of excess enthusiasm, as for want of a better.

It looks as if the breeder wanted a rose for cut flower growers, because the flowers are usually borne singly on straight stems, like the roses one buys from the florist.

19

MISCHIEF

Hybrid Tea

Grown for the fine quality of its freely produced blooms, which are pink with a tint of coral. The flowers, of about 28 petals, open to a regular circular outline, with the pointed center holding to a late stage. The end-of-season blooms are usually shaded orange. The compact, leafy bushes make a good solid bed.

The foliage, however, lacks sparkle; and although usually considered fragrant, 'Mischief' looks as if it should be more scented than it actually is.

Raised by Sam McGredy in Northern Ireland from 'Peace' × 'Spartan,' and introduced in 1961, this rose had a great reception in Britain, where it has continued as a leading variety.

The general criticism accuses it of being susceptible to rust; and it should be avoided in places where that disease is troublesome. But people can be found who consider other roses a greater rust risk.

20

MAINZER FASTNACHT
syn BLUE MOON

Hybrid Tea

A blue rose? Well, the nearest we have to it with large and well-formed blooms. The color is really a pink which looks rather blue, and it varies considerably according to the light it is grown or viewed in. It is an interesting rose, well worth growing; and those who shiver at "blue" roses can at least enjoy the powerful sweet scent.

There are about 38 petals. The plants are upright, adequate without being robust.

Raised in Germany by Mathias Tantau from two unnamed seedlings, 'Blue Moon' was introduced in 1964. Its name in France is 'Sissi.' Although there are other roses of this color, it has so far been rated higher than any of them in just about every part of the world.

Despite such advances as this rose undoubtedly is, the true blue color in roses is no nearer for it, as far as can be judged. It is a variation on red, not a break into blue.

21

MICHÈLE MEILLAND

Hybrid Tea

A slim and graceful rose, making out of its pale flowers and dark stems as handsome a bush as any Hybrid Tea. The buds are pearl pink, and open into rather small flowers exquisitely shaped, hiding tints of pink and amber until they open. These tints are variable, for 'Michèle Meilland' can look quite different from one season to another. The flower stems bear few thorns, often none at all. This pleasant bush, unobtrusive, and yet so useful in the garden and for cutting, should appeal to all except those who demand vivid colors and large blooms.

It was raised in France by Francis Meilland from 'Joanna Hill' × 'Peace' and introduced in 1945. It has been grown and loved in most countries, and if latterly it has lost some support, the fault lies with the world's restless quest for change, not with 'Michèle Meilland.'

A precious pearl of a rose, good for cutting.

22

OPHELIA

Hybrid Tea

The oldest Hybrid Tea in general cultivation—and why? For its sweet center, sweet scent, and easy growth. The color is blush, almost white, with a touch of yellow. The flowers are not large, but stand up straight, often in great clusters. They have about 28 petals, the outer ones slow to bend away from the cherished heart. The bushes are homely and easy, with modest pretty leaves, slightly blue-green. The flowers are good to cut.

The only failing is that the sepals do not obstruct thunderflies from getting into the buds.

'Ophelia' was raised in England and introduced in 1912 by William Paul, who confessed ignorance of how it arose. It has been loved all round the world by two generations. Of the many sports from it, 'Mme Butterfly' and 'Lady Sylvia' are the best known.

The one sported to the other; in the same line is 'Rapture,' deeper pink.

23

MOJAVE

Hybrid Tea

Color is 'Mojave's' attraction, a reddish orange color, with the flowers held up on the top of the bushes, like many birds of bright plumage perched on slim stalks. The flowers are fairly small, with about 25 petals, opening from pointed young buds, soon expanding to show their centers.

Although the vivid orange red color of the young flowers is somewhat crimsoned and muted in the old, it is still remarkable. The bushes grow upright, and after a few years are more apt than most to look gaunt. No use smelling 'Mojave,' unless your nose is keen.

This rose was raised in California by Herbert Swim, from 'Charlotte Armstrong' × 'Signora,' and introduced by Armstrong Nurseries in 1954. It is rated as good in the United States and grown with pleasure nearly all over the world.

There is no better rose in this color as yet.

24

NATIONAL TRUST
syn BAD NAUHEIM

Hybrid Tea

It is brilliant red, all sparkle in flower, and gleam in foliage, growing low for a Hybrid Tea. Therefore this rose is tailor-made for many a spot where a high-quality red of short stature is required. The flowers are well formed, not of great expanse, but of more substance than one might suppose, having a good 50 petals. The red color holds extremely well.

This agreeable rose is "for your *eyes* only," and not for your *nose.*

It was bred in Northern Ireland by Sam McGredy from 'Evelyn Fison' × 'King of Hearts' and introduced in 1970. A popular rose in Britain and Germany, it is rated good in the United States, and is moving up in international circles.

After a few years in general currency, it is soon discovered whether roses are healthy or not. 'National Trust' has a good health record, and thus is likely to prosper.

25

PASCALI

Hybrid Tea

The gardener who would plant only one white rose should choose this one, for it is a fine garden rose and one of the best for cutting. The blooms are substantial, but not so large as to lose their grace. The 30 petals are firmly entwined at the base, to enclose a sweet cone of a heart, slightly creamy, and to hold it firm longer than most roses can manage. The stems are long and straight, the bush of good proportions.

Only in its meager fragrance does this rose disappoint.

It was raised in Belgium by Louis Lens, from 'Queen Elizabeth' × 'White Butterfly,' and introduced in 1963; it reached America in 1968. It had a rapturous reception all over Europe, Britain being meanest; it is rated excellent in America and in virtually all rose-growing countries.

It is certainly the best rose raised by Louis Lens, and probably the best ever produced by a Belgian.

26

PEACE syn GLORIA DEI,
Mme A. MEILLAND

Hybrid Tea

The world's favorite rose, according to a poll in 1976. It inspired the book, *For Love of a Rose,* by Antonia Ridge. It is the modern legend of roses, the watershed of the 1940s, the rose nobody dreamed of before it came; but now (such is man's ingratitude) it is thought quite commonplace. It is light yellow, beautifully edged and shaded pink, wide, enormous. Its 40 petals, big ones, form a flower that is as handsome fully blown as in all its other lovely stages. It is a strong, vigorous bush, taller and wider than average.

One can fault it for lack of scent, but Scrooge himself must be called in to find further complaints.

It was raised in France by Francis Meilland, and introduced in 1942 as 'Mme A. Meilland'; the Conard-Pyle Company introduced it in the United States in 1945 as 'Peace.' The quoted parents are Seedling × 'Margaret McGredy.' But this is not certain.

27

PINK FAVORITE

Hybrid Tea

The flowers are deep pink, bold and big, held by stalks of appropriate stoutness above a shining sea of clean-cut leaves. It looks the picture of health, and usually is. The normal 28 petals stretch from fat buds into large flowers, gloriously high-centered and symmetrical.

This solid, masculine sort of rose is fine for the garden and cutting; it is not very fragrant.

It was raised by Gordon von Abrams in California from 'Juno' × Seedling and was introduced by Peterson and Dering of Scapoose, Oregon, in 1956. The Americans rate it good; the British vote it one of the best; it is grown in most countries, but seems to find little favor over much of Europe, and still less in Australia.

An interesting fact of its parentage is that one grandparent was the popular climbing 'New Dawn.' Possibly that is how 'Pink Favorite' got its health, vigor, and glossy leaves.

28

PICCADILLY

Hybrid Tea

Roses are quite ready to manufacture different colors, one to adorn the inner surface of the petal, and another to coat the outer. Of the contrasts thus made, red against yellow is the most gaudy, and few varieties show it more freely than 'Piccadilly.' The shiny dark leaves assist well in the glittering effect.
The flowers are large, well formed with about 25 petals; the color is most vivid when young, and less scarlet but still pleasing when fully expanded. The bushes are compact, slightly below average height, not always long-lived.
Sam McGredy raised it in Northern Ireland from 'McGredy's Yellow' × 'Karl Herbst' and introduced it in 1960.
Although rated only fair in the United States, it has had a distinguished international career.
The breeder no doubt named it for the bright lights of Piccadilly Circus; its stamens and stigmas, like Eros, are in the center.

29

PEEP O' DAY

Hybrid Tea

This rose had an unusual career, because the author sent it to the firm of Frank Mason & Son in New Zealand, and subsequently lost it himself. Alan Mason found it to be a pure and clean color, with much of the charm of 'Michèle Meilland,' but more lustrous. It starts clear pink with a touch of apricot and expands glowing apricot. The plants, of average height, spread out well and achieve, in Mr. Mason's words, 'massive production,' partly because the flowering times come in quick succession. He recommends that it be generously fed, to encourage (or reward?) its performance.
'Peep o' Day' has subsequently become one of New Zealand's favorites, and it is invading Australia too. It was raised by the author from ('Pink Parfait' × 'Highlight') × 'Orion,' and introduced in New Zealand in 1973. Stock was subsequently sent back from New Zealand.

30

RED DEVIL
syn CŒUR D'AMOUR

Hybrid Tea

Anyone can grow flowers of champion size by planting 'Red Devil,' because it produces the kind of show-stoppers usually expected only from experts. The plants are big too, about the size of 'Peace.' The way to encourage the largest possible blooms is to leave one bud to a stem, by breaking out the side buds as soon as they are big enough to handle.
Then may come an enormous flower, light red, perfumed, with 60 or 70 petals opening to show a pure straight heart and a regular outline. Even those who don't like their roses to imitate cabbages can scarce forebear to cheer.
It comes from Northern Ireland, where Patrick Dickson raised it from 'Silver Lining' × Seedling and introduced it in 1967. Jackson and Perkins brought it out in America in 1970, and now it is grown internationally, especially by the keen showmen. It wins them medals galore.

31

PRECIOUS PLATINUM
syn RED STAR

Hybrid Tea

This relative newcomer has swiftly made its name for scintillating rich red flowers; these blooms, backed by leaves which glisten with well-being, are held on high by a tall, vigorous plant. The result is a red parade visible a long way off.
Individually the blooms are formed of about 35 petals, the outer ones soon opening from the heart, which itself is slow to unfold. There is not much scent.
Patrick Dickson raised it in Northern Ireland from 'Red Planet' × 'Franklin Engelmann.' Introduced in 1974, within four years it was being enthusiastically grown in Britain, France, America, Germany, and Australia, with other countries taking a keen interest too.
'Red Star' is the name in France, Belgium, Switzerland, and Italy; 'Opa Pötschke' in Germany; it may yet appear in Scandinavia and elsewhere under a fourth name.

A WORLD OF ROSES

THE TWENTY-ONE PRINCIPAL TYPES

The rich variety of the rose genus is indicated in the three types pictured here:

'Shot Silk' (above) belongs to the most popular class today, the high-centered, many-petaled Hybrid Teas.

Much more like a wild rose is 'Frühlingsmorgen' (right), a Scotch rose, which is single (five-petaled), with plentiful blossoms.

'Königin von Danemarck' (below), a double Alba, is intricately formed.

The favorite rose of the modern world is a high-centered flower growing by itself on a thorny stem; in other words, a Hybrid Tea, of which the most famous example is 'Mme A. Meilland,' or as she is generally known, 'Peace.' But it was not always thus. In the long history of the rose there have been many fashions in favorites, and we cannot suppose that history having reached our time will stand still; on the contrary, it is more likely to move faster than ever.

The Hybrid Tea, so popular today, took its rise from about the middle of the nineteenth century; its particular blend of form and size was unknown before. Yet the rose had been called the Queen of Flowers for the preceding two thousand years at least. And it follows that the genus contained from the beginning beauties as satisfying to previous generations as 'Peace' is to us.

It would be a grievous loss not to appreciate those beauties, to blind ourselves to all but one ephemeral type; for in doing so, we should lose the history of the past, the charming alternatives of the present, and the resources placed ready to build the roses of the future.

The world of roses extends not only geographically to every place on the earth where roses grow, but through time, and into human consciousness. Geography cannot describe that world, because roses care nothing for frontiers; time cannot divide roses into various reigns or periods, because whatever roses the ancient Greeks or Romans bred may be repeated today.

But human consciousness is another matter, because it is the relativity of roses to mankind that causes this book to be written, published, and read. Therefore in the next pages are encapsulated most of the known types of roses which have captivated gardeners in the past and present. We include a necessarily brief note on their appearance and origin, and lists of the leading varieties, usually in order of preference, to guide those who wish to grow any of these types of roses in their best and highest expression.

This chapter presents a survey of the most important types of roses, from the wild flowers of antiquity to the latest trend, the Miniatures.

On the following pages, one rose from each type is illustrated in a photograph. The rose pictured in each case is marked with an asterisk (*) in the list to the right of the photograph.

41

WILD ROSES

R. moyesii *'Geranium'*;
R. ecae *'Golden Chersonese'*;
R. xanthina *'Canary Bird'*; R.
virginiana; R. x high-
downensis; R. webbiana; R.
rubrifolia; R. macrophylla
'Doncasterii'; R. farreri per-
setosa; R. moyesii *'Fred
Streeter'*; R. x pruhoniciana;
R. roxburghii normalis;
R. willmottiae; R. nitida;
R. helenae; R. filipes *'Kifts-
gate'*;* R. foetida bicolor;
R. x cantabrigiensis; R.
sericea pteracantha; R. ecae;
R. moyesii; R. pomifera; R.
foetida; R. stellata mirifica.

Wild roses are either shrubs or climbers; and all those listed here are shrubs, except for *R. helenae* and *R. filipes* 'Kiftsgate,' which are climbers well suited to grow through trees. Most of the shrubs occupy considerable space and should be planted a meter (1 yard) apart or more, except *R. nitida* and *R. stellata mirifica,* which are relatively small.
The flowers are normally produced once in the year, with *R. ecae* 'Golden Chersonese' leading the way in late spring, and *R. virginiana* after mid-summer; but many of them produce beautiful hips in autumn, especially the types of *R. moyesii* and *R. macrophylla.*
The variations in leaves, thorns, flower colors, and scent will prove fascinating to anyone who takes an interest in nature at all. These wild roses include natives of China, Central Asia, Europe, and North America; grouped in a border, they can bring the natural wonders of the rose world together in a single garden.

BANKSIANS etc.

*The famous Banksian Yellow
is the double-flowered
R. banksiae lutea; there is
also a double white, R. banksiae alba-plena; of less horticultural attraction are the
single yellow and white, respectively R. banksiae lutescens
and normalis. Closely related
is R. laevigata,* the Cherokee
Rose, of which there is a pink
hybrid called R. X
anemonoides, and a red sport
from it, 'Ramona.' The Macartney Rose is also related; it is
R. bracteata, of which the
most famous hybrid is the
lovely climber 'Mermaid.'*

All these roses are climbers, and they are among the five rose species which share one unique factor: their stipules are not properly joined to the leafstalk, but only attached by their base. Indeed the stipules often fall off soon after the leaves are mature. This recognition factor applies to the species, but not necessarily to hybrids such as 'Mermaid,' because of the influence of the other parent involved.
The origin of all these roses is Chinese, for even the Cherokee Rose comes from that country, although it is so firmly naturalized in the United States that it is the emblem of the state of Georgia. Of its two hybrids, the pink one was raised in Germany and the red in California. Neither of these hybrids has proved to be perfectly hardy.
The Macartney Rose has overlapping green bracts growing even on the sepals; its wonderful hybrid 'Mermaid' was raised in England in 1918 and is still to be seen on countless home walls.

HYBRID CHINAS

*'Cécile Brunner' (the Sweet-
heart Rose), obtainable both
as bush or a climber; 'Old
Blush,' an original import
from China; the Green Rose,
R. chinensis viridiflora, its
petals as if made from leaf;
R. chinensis mutabilis,* famous for its utter color change;
'Fortune's Double Yellow,'
not hardy, an orange yellow
climber found in Ningpo in
1842; 'Perle d'Or'; 'Serratipetala'; 'Miss Lowe's Variety';
'Hermosa'; 'Fellemberg';
R. chinensis semperflorens;
'Fabvier'; 'Cramoisi
Supérieur.'*

The China roses were developed long before they came out of that country during the eighteenth and nineteenth centuries; some people suggest they may be a thousand years old, but there is no certainty of it. The first varieties known to Europeans were purchased from Chinese gardens and nurseries from about 1752, which is the date given for 'Old Blush' reaching Sweden. That rose, and *R. chinensis semperflorens,* 'Hume's Blush Tea-Scented China,' and 'Parks' Yellow Tea-Scented China,' were the four important Chinese varieties destined to change completely the roses of the west. Their most important attribute was remontancy, that is, the ability to flower twice or oftener in a season. They also brought their own fresh scent, different from the heavier fragrance of western roses; their clean-cut, bright leaves were to give a sparkle to the dull foliage of western roses; and with *R. chinensis semperflorens* came a true red color, without the purple look of our old red roses.

NOISETTES

These Victorian roses have mostly faded away, but some are still grown and loved: 'Mme Alfred Carrière,' white; 'William Allen Richardson,' orange-yellow; 'Gloire de Dijon,'* buff yellow; 'Aimée Vibert,' white; 'Céline Forestier,' light yellow; 'Desprez à Fleur Jaune,' pale yellow. These are all climbers. The most famous of all is 'Maréchal Niel,' one of the most beautiful yellow roses ever seen. Unfortunately it is now rare, because of its tenderness and diminished vigor. It was not only yellow, but scented.

The Noisettes originated in Charleston, South Carolina, through the China 'Old Blush' being grown near to the wild Musk Rose, *R. moschata.* Seed from one of these two was sown, and because the resulting seedling had the Musk habit of climbing, with the pink color of the China, it was assumed to be a hybrid and introduced as 'Champney's Pink Cluster.' It flowered, like the Musk Rose, only in the summer.

When in turn seed was taken from 'Champney's Pink Cluster' by nurseryman Philippe Noisette in Charleston, it yielded proof of the mating, because the next generation was remontant. Philippe's seedling became famous as 'Blush Noisette.' 'Blush Noisette' when crossed with 'Parks' Yellow Tea-scented China' set the pattern of Noisettes in the form of a white climber called 'Lamarque'; but before the nineteenth century was out, hardier roses were called for, and the Noisette strain was merged with others.

TEAS

The hardiest and most easily grown Teas are the apricot yellow 'Lady Hillingdon'* and the white 'Mrs. Herbert Stevens'; both are also available as climbers. Apart from these, only a specialist should attempt Teas. The famous varieties of the past were 'Safrano,' saffron marked red; the white 'Niphetos,' which is Greek for snowy, and of which there was a climber too; 'Devoniensis,' creamy white, more easily found in its climbing form; 'Perle des Jardins'; and 'Général Schablikine,' red and hardy, but with small flowers.

Tea was an abbreviation for Tea-scented China roses; and to rosarians of the nineteenth century, they were the aristocrats of roses. They have been superseded by Hybrid Teas. However, they are an important stage in the history of the modern rose and are still affectionately preserved by enthusiasts in suitable climates, such as in the south of both Europe and the United States, the Canary Islands, and Bermuda. In frosty countries, Teas can be grown only under glass.

They are directly descended from two varieties imported from that country in the early nineteenth century. There has been much speculation as to how the Chinese got them, with the general conclusion favoring a marriage between the China Rose and *R. gigantea.* The latter is a large white climbing rose, wild in south China and Burma.

The class began about 1830, with a variety called 'Mme Roussel,' and the last good Teas came out in 1910, notably 'Lady Hillingdon.'

HYBRID TEAS

'Pascali,' white; 'Red Devil'; 'Silver Jubilee,' pink blend; 'Wendy Cussons,' carmine; 'Alexander,' vermilion; 'Grandpa Dickson syn Irish Gold'; 'Alec's Red'; 'Dr. A.J. Verhage syn Golden Wave'; 'Duftwolke syn Fragrant Cloud,' red; 'Just Joey,' coppery buff; 'Sonia Meilland syn Sweet Promise,' pink; 'Precious Platinum syn Red Star'; 'Mme A. Meilland syn Peace,' yellow and pink; 'Ophelia,' blush; 'National Trust syn Bad Nauheim,' red; 'Mischief,' pink; 'First Love,' pink; 'John Waterer,' red.

The tender Teas were crossbred with the tough Hybrid Perpetuals, giving a class of roses more beautiful and useful than either. The first generally acknowledged variety was 'La France,' a pink rose introduced in 1867. To the end of the nineteenth century, Hybrid Teas improved in their beauty and freedom of flower. A great development occurred in 1900, when Joseph Pernet-Ducher introduced 'Soleil d'Or,' and with it the color derived from a completely different rose, 'Persian Yellow.' This accession of a new color diversified the class, which continued in a fairly set pattern of growth, via 'Ophelia' in 1912, 'Shot Silk' in 1924, 'Mrs. Sam McGredy'* in 1929, and 'Ena Harkness' in 1946.

The growth received a fillip in 1942, from 'Mme A. Meilland,' otherwise 'Peace'; Wilhelm Kordes of Germany led Hybrid Musks and Sweet Briars into the blood stream; many other breeders have also played their parts in maintaining the vitality of this class for over a century.

FLORIBUNDAS

'Allgold,'* yellow; 'Queen Elizabeth,' pink; 'Schnee-wittchen syn Iceberg,' white; 'Pink Parfait'; 'Europeana,' crimson; 'Southampton,' apricot orange; 'Arthur Bell,' yellow; 'Prominent syn Korp,' vermilion; 'Margaret Merril,' blush; 'Anne Cocker,' vermilion; 'Escapade,' rosy violet; 'Marlena,' crimson; 'Rob Roy,' crimson; 'Circus,' yellow and red; 'Lili Marlene,' scarlet; 'Sarabande,' scarlet; 'Anne Harkness syn Harkaramel,' amber yellow. There are also climbing Floribundas, especially 'Golden Showers'; 'Handel.'

The ideal Hybrid Tea puts the strength of a whole shoot into one flower; but most roses naturally produce many flowers upon one shoot, and one species which is actually named on account of that propensity is *R. multiflora*. From it and the Chinas was bred a race of small-flowered bedding roses called Polyanthas; and no sooner were these in existence, than breeders sought to make their flowers larger by crossing them with Hybrid Teas.

The pioneers in this work were the Poulsens in Denmark; Le Grice and Prior in England, and Kordes in Germany followed; and Eugene Boerner in the United States set the fashion of double Floribundas. Everyone can see the advantage of bushes which bear beautiful flowers in great abundance—the hallmark of a Floribunda. However, there are physical limitations as to the size and number of blooms a bush can accommodate, and these are the factors which draw a line between Floribundas and Hybrid Teas.

HYBRID MUSKS

'Cornelia,' pink, large wide bush; 'Moonlight,' cream, tall with shiny leaves; 'Buff Beauty,' double, biscuit color; 'Penelope,' light pink to near white; 'Prosperity,' small double flowers, ivory; 'Felicia,' light pink; 'Vanity,' single, deep pink, so leggy it is best grown as a climber, but attractive with its silky flowers; 'Wilhelm syn Skyrocket,' red, of rather more Floribunda character; 'Will Scarlet,'* a bright red sport of 'Wilhelm'; 'Francesca,' single, ivory slightly shaded apricot; 'Danaë,' ivory.

This is a small and not clearly defined class of shrub roses. The originator was the Reverend Joseph Pemberton, a priest in the Church of England, who resigned the ministry after thirty-four years, in order to spend the evening of his life growing roses. Having raised a number of handsome varieties, he called them Hybrid Musks, because they did not fit easily into any of the classes of the time, which was approximately 1920. This was a fortunate name for him, because the Musk Rose had a great reputation for perfume, and was a name familiar to everyone out of literature, even though very few people knew what it looked like. In fact, Pemberton's Hybrid Musks owed far more to Polyanthas, Teas, and Hybrid Teas than ever to the Musk. In character many are like strong, wide-growing semi-double Floribundas and were used as bedding plants before the Floribundas became so good. It is more common nowadays to grow them as shrubs on their own, or as part of a rose hedge.

MINIATURES

'Rosina syn Josephine Wheatcroft,' yellow; 'Pour Toi,' white; 'New Penny,' pink; 'Easter Morning,' white; 'Baby Masquerade,' yellow and pink; 'Starina,' orange scarlet; 'Darling Flame syn Minuetto,' orange vermilion; 'Cinderella,' blush white; 'Judy Fischer,' pink; 'Toy Clown,' white tipped pink; 'Mr. Bluebird,' purple; less typical varieties, but interesting, are 'Little Flirt,'* carmine and yellow, large flowers; 'Dresden Doll,' pink with mossy buds; 'Perla de Alcanada,' red, pompon flowers.

These appealing little roses appear to have begun as undersized seedlings from the red *R. chinensis semperflorens;* or in other words as an unexpected natural development from the Crimson China. They were first described in the early nineteenth century, with some uncertainty as to the place of origin, which is usually said to have been Mauritius.

They were popular as pot plants in the flower markets of England and France in the nineteenth century, but virtually disappeared toward the end of it and were rediscovered about 1918, when Colonel Roulet observed a few old plants growing in pots in a Swiss village. The variety he saw was introduced in 1922 as 'Rouletii'; it was crossed with Polyanthas by De Vink of Holland, and with Hybrid Teas by Dot of Spain, to usher in the many varieties in vogue today.

They may be grown as garden or pot plants, but they are not natural indoor subjects; they may be brought into the home while in flower, and should then go outside again.

POLYANTHAS

Modern Polyanthas are not necessarily small plants, for example, 'Ballerina,'* light pink; 'Yesterday syn Tapis d'Orient,' pink; 'Marjorie Fair,' red; 'Mozart,' light pink; and the older 'Robin Hood,' red. The older varieties of shorter habit include 'Marie Pavié,' pale pink; 'Ellen Poulsen,' pink; 'Gloria Mundi,' orange vermilion (but it reverts); and the stumpy but amazing amethyst 'Baby Faurax.' Many climbing Polyanthas were raised and are very beautiful, including 'Goldfinch,' yellow to white.

R. multiflora is a hardy wild rose from east China, Korea, and Japan; although not particularly beautiful, having dull, rough leaves and small white flowers, it has given much to garden roses—its large heads of small blooms, and an extraordinary readiness to break into strange colors. From this unspectacular species have arisen some of the most impressive purple and geranium red colors. The first Polyanthas were introduced in France about 1875, from crosses generally accepted to have been between seedlings of *R. multiflora* and Chinas. They were the first roses to qualify as short, remontant bedding plants, and therefore opened up whole new areas of gardens to the rose.

In the period up to about 1935 Polyanthas were indispensable bedding roses, but Floribundas have almost completely taken their place. It would be a pity to lose them entirely, because plants bearing innumerable diminutive flowers offer a charm and beauty all their own.

WICHURAIANA HYBRIDS

'Sander's White'; 'Crimson Shower'; 'New Dawn,' blush; 'Albertine,'* pink; 'Alberic Barbier,' cream yellow; 'May Queen,' pink; 'Jersey Beauty,' cream; 'Emily Gray,' yellow; 'Dr. W. van Fleet,' blush. Particularly beautiful is a bush variety, 'The Fairy,' pink. The 'Dorothy Perkins' type accommodate too many mildew spores to be recommended. Of the Kordesii: 'Leverkusen,' yellow; 'Parkdirektor Riggers,' crimson; 'Ritter von Barmstede,' pink. Wichuraiana blood is appearing in many "ground cover" roses.

R. wichuraiana is the Memorial Rose, so called because it was used in the United States to plant on graves, which it then covered with long shoots trailing upon the ground. Its dark shiny leaves are a perfect foil to the starry white flowers. It is a wild rose from China, Korea, and Japan. First American, and then French breeders used it to create the roses known for many years as ramblers; which is a rather indefinite name for climbing roses of a trailing habit, usually flowering only in summer.

The types produced varied considerably; for example, Teas and Hybrid Teas would tend to give flowers of the type of 'Albertine' and 'New Dawn,' while Polyanthas were no doubt responsible for the smaller flowers of 'Dorothy Perkins' and 'Excelsa.'

Some of the hybrids were bushes, not climbers; and a more recent development, perhaps deserving a class of its own, are the Kordesii roses, bred from a hybrid of *R. rugosa* and *R. wichuraiana.*

GALLICAS

R. gallica versicolor *syn* 'Rosa Mundi,' red striped blush; 'Tuscany,' maroon red; 'Tuscany Superb,' maroon red, more double than 'Tuscany'; 'Cardinal de Richelieu,' purple; 'Gloire de France,' pink; 'Belle de Crécy,' slate pink to mauve; 'Charles de Mills,'* crimson; 'Président de Sèze,' purple and pink; 'Surpasse Tout,' red; 'Camaieux,' purple striped blush; R. gallica officinalis, red; 'Duc de Guiche,' crimson. Related to the Gallicas is the pink shrub R. x francofurtana, *pleasantly fragrant.*

These are probably the oldest garden roses cultivated in the West, and consequently much loved by connoisseurs of old roses. But it should be clearly understood that it is the *type* which is old, not necessarily the *varieties.* All through history, the varieties most probably changed, and most of the old roses grown today were raised in the nineteenth century. The oldest ones in this list appear to be *R. gallica versicolor* syn 'Rosa Mundi,' about 1650, and 'Tuscany,' possibly earlier. Our varieties *may* have been similar to those of ancient times.

R. gallica is a native of western Asia and the more temperate parts of Europe. Its natural variations from pink to red, and from single to semi-double, led to the selection of varieties. And its uses in medicine were important in medieval times; *R. gallica officinalis* was called the Apothecary's Rose.

The Gallicas flower only in summer and are prone to mildew; the colors seem somewhat bizarre today.

DAMASKS

Not a great many varieties survive from the hundreds of the past. The most beautiful is 'Madame Hardy,' double white. 'Quatre Saisons' is a historic item, sharp pink, very fragrant, known from old as the 'Four Seasons Rose'; there is an interesting sport from it, a white Moss, called 'Quatre Saisons Blanc Mousseux'; 'Celsiana'* is pink, becoming white, very fragrant; R. X damascena trigintipetala, not much of a garden rose, is the main variety used for Attar of Roses; 'La Ville de Bruxelles,' pink.

The origin of the Damasks is hidden in the mists of time, and the first firm evidence declares their existence in Italy in the early 1500s. It is probable they are older, possible they are nearly as old as the Gallicas. The name may point to their place of origin, but on the other hand 'Austrian Yellow' stands as an example of a misleading identity of this nature.

Damasks are usually tall shrubs with an open habit, which can be untidy as their branches arch outward. They have pale colors, pink or white, and flower only in summer, with the notable exception of 'Quatre Saisons,' which was for years the only remontant rose in the West, and is probably the most ancient of the surviving varieties. How that rose evolved is a mystery, but the theory for Damasks in general is that they came from R. gallica and some wild climbing rose, possibly R. phoenicia. Damasks have for centuries been cultivated by the producers of Attar of Roses.

CENTIFOLIAS

'Bullata,' pink, has the typical flower, also wrinkled leaves; 'Chapeau de Napoléon syn Crested Moss' has a poor pink flower, but a marvelous cockade growth on the buds; 'Fantin-Latour'* is blush, with flowers as in old paintings; 'Robert le Diable' is purple-pink, not the easiest of growers; 'Tour de Malakoff' has wide, untypical growth, with smoky pink flowers, not everyone's taste. There are several varieties with pink pompon flowers, small and attractive, especially 'Petite de Hollande' and the compact 'Spong.'

These have been known as Cabbage Roses, Provence Roses, Holland Roses, and Hundred-petaled Roses in various times and places. "Cabbage" means that the center petals fold over the stigmas and stamens; it has nothing to do with size. "Provence" and "Holland" refer to the two rival claims of origin. "Hundred-petaled" refers to the Latin name, Centifolia; it is not meant to be an exact count. Centifolias are by no means roses of antiquity upon the available evidence, which dates them from about 1550, when it appears likely they were raised in Holland. The idea of their greater age arises from the fact that ancient Greek and Roman writers described a "hundred-petaled" rose.

They are in appearance a halfway stage between Gallicas and Damasks, more upright and leggy than Gallicas, but more compact than Damasks. They flower in summer and usually have double flowers, with the outside petals expanded about a low and rounded center.

MOSSES

The best is easily 'Common Moss,'* also known as 'Old Pink Moss' or just 'Pink Moss.' It is taken by some experts to have been the first one, and if so, it was never bettered. From it came some good white sports, variously sold as 'Shailer's White Moss,' 'White Moss,' or 'White Bath,' probably indistinguishable. Do not mistake these for 'Blanche Moreau,' which has dark moss of lesser appeal. 'Général Kléber,' pink; 'Henri Martin,' red; two purple varieties are worth growing for their color, 'Laneii' and 'William Lobb.'

Moss roses are descendants from the Centifolias, originally sports. Other types of roses can produce mossy growth on their seedpods and sepals, as happened long ago in the Damasks, and only recently with the Miniatures. Those types are usually referred to their own classes, this one being kept more or less as our great-grandparents knew it. Moss roses apparently originated about 1700. The mossy growth about the flower bud seems to be a modification of little bristles, and at its best it ends in a small frond like a wisp of moss. This is a charming embellishment, lost from view of course as soon as the flower opens. Therefore the beauty of Moss roses is in the buds, rather than as garden plants. They flower in summer.

Of the many varieties which have been introduced, only a few are remarkably mossy; for it unfortunately became the habit to class anything with a bristly seedpod as a Moss, on the grounds that Centifolias were smoother.

BOURBONS

'Souvenir de la Malmaison,' blush white, most beautiful (there is a climber, not so remontant, and a lovely single sport, 'Souvenir de St. Anne's'); 'Boule de Neige,' white, very double; 'Mme Pierre Oger,' pink, dainty as a seashell, but may get blackspot; 'Zéphirine Drouhin,' the favorite pink "thornless" climber, foliage dull for the class; 'Kathleen Harrop,' a paler 'Zéphirine Drouhin'; 'Gloire des Rosomanes,' well known as 'Ragged Robin,' a rangy red rose; 'Mme Isaac Pereire,'* pink.

An important class of the nineteenth century, giving evidence of a clear step on the way from old roses to new. In it, the dull foliage of the old western roses accepted a gleam from the eastern, and the petals became larger, more separated, luminous. This rose was probably discovered in the island of Réunion (then the Île de Bourbon) in the Indian Ocean. It was among a plantation of 'Old Blush' that fecund pink China rose, and 'Duchess of Portland,' which was reckoned to have descended from the Damask 'Quatre Saisons.' Seeds were sent to France in 1819, and in a very short time gave rise to varieties so distinct as to be grouped as Bourbon roses. There is, however, some question as to whether parallel events occurred in Mauritius and in India. The class gave way to Hybrid Perpetuals, but some of the survivors are certainly worth growing today. In countries where spring frosts are common, the summer flowers are often spoiled in consequence, and the autumn blooms may be better.

HYBRID PERPETUALS

Only specialists would grow Hybrid Perpetuals, apart from one famous and beloved variety, the white 'Frau Karl Druschki syn Snow Queen.' It was introduced in 1900, and despite its occasional touch of pink, it remains the purest white rose to this day. An interesting variety, but with a smaller flower of quite different form, is 'Roger Lambelin':* its dark red petals are edged white. There is also a very fine pink, 'Mrs. John Laing,' with broad flowers of regal form. Notable for color is 'Reine des Violettes.'

From the Bourbons and lesser-known types of roses, about 1830 a class began to emerge with a mixture of features, but with the common factor of being remontant. It was eventually given the ambitious name Hybrid Perpetual, under which it laid hold of the hearts of rosarians, inspired them to grow roses, to show them, to form rose societies. As the century progressed, Teas were bred into the class, and thus the final step toward the modern rose was taken; for the first Hybrid Tea appeared in 1867, and by the end of the century, Hybrid Perpetuals were on their way out.

Although there are only a few Hybrid Perpetuals worth growing today, it is well to acknowledge the great influence of the class. The size of the blooms, which some might consider coarse, was a revelation in their day; their solidity made them ideal for showing, because many varieties held their form for days without blowing open. They set the scene for our rose world.

SCOTCH ROSES

'Andrewsii,' cream pink, semi-double, short; 'Double White,' short; 'Falkland,' soft pink, semi-double, short; 'Frühlingsgold,' primrose, semi-double, large shrub; 'Frühlingsmorgen,' single, pink, tall; 'Golden Wings,' cream yellow, single, tall, remontant; 'Harisonii,'* yellow, double, gaunt; 'Lutea,' yellow, single, medium height; 'Marguerite Hilling,' pink, single, tall, spectacular; 'Mrs. Colville,' purple, semi-double, short; 'Nevada,' white, single, tall, spectacular; R. spinosissima hispida, cream white.

Scotch roses are descended from *R. spinosissima,* one of the hardiest of wild roses. It is also a fruitful rose, breeding quite readily with many garden varieties. Therefore the accompanying list contains some diverse roses. The true Scotch roses are low, compact, suckering shrubs, flowering only in late spring, and to this group belong 'Andrewsii,' 'Double White,' 'Falkland,' 'Lutea,' Mrs. Colville, 'William III,' and 'Williams' Double Yellow.' Two wild varieties from Siberia and Mongolia are *R. spinosissima altaica* and *hispida;* they are taller and more open in habit than the species and have handsome black hips. From them, or other parents, are the interesting and in some cases historic varieties which complete the list, most of them large shrubs when compared with the low prototypes of the class. Beginners' choice of old Scotch roses: 'Stanwell Perpetual,' 'William III,' 'Williams' Double Yellow'; and of the lovely later hybrids, 'Golden Wings' and 'Marguerite Hilling.'

ALBAS

'Celestial,' light rose, double; 'Mme Legras de St. Germain,' white, double; 'Félicité Parmentier,' pink and white, double; 'Maiden's Blush,' blush white, double, of which two forms are offered, the Great and the Small, the difference being the size of the bushes; 'Pompon Blanc Parfait,' white, double; 'Königin von Danemarck,' pink, double; 'Semi-plena,'* white, semi-double, the only one with good hips; 'Belle Amour,' pink, semi-double; 'Blush Hip,' light pink, semi-double; 'Chloris,' blush, double.

Albas are fine upstanding shrubs with handsome leaves, and a color range limited to white and light pink. They flower only in the summer, but the intricate flower forms of most of them show all the delights we expect from old fashioned roses including Damasks and Gallicas as well as the Albas.

And these are truly old, some of the most senior roses of the west, their origin unknown. Most of the varieties listed here were raised in the eighteenth and nineteenth centuries, but it is generally thought that the class goes back to classical times. The summer display is a feast of roses, while the fine gray-green foliage, resistant to blackspot, keeps the shrubs handsome to leaf-fall. They are delightful plants to grow, as vigorous and easy as they are fragrant and beautiful. The height and spread are considerable; most will grow head high or more.

The supposition is that they originated from a cross between a Damask and a Dog Rose, long, long ago.

EGLANTERIA HYBRIDS

'Lady Penzance,' prawn pink with yellow, single; 'Fritz Nobis,' pink, double, no leaf scent; 'Amy Robsart,' pink, semi-double; 'Anne of Geierstein,' crimson, single; 'Catherine Seyton,' pink, single; 'Janet's Pride,' pink and white, semi-double; 'Julia Mannering,' pearl, single; 'Lord Penzance,' fawn pink with yellow, single; 'Lucy Ashton,' white-edged pink, single; 'Meg Merrilies,'* carmine, single; 'Rosenwunder,' crimson, semi-double. Most of the above are also known as Penzance Sweet Briars.

These are the Sweet Briars, grown not so much for their flowers as for the apple-like scent of their leaves. The glands do not emit their scent without being bruised, which is done most effectively by rain. The humid atmosphere normally following a summer shower is ideal for the fragrance to spread far and wide. The wild Sweet Briar is *R. eglanteria* (formerly *R. rubiginosa*); it has many sharp prickles, light pink flowers, and fine red hips; not unlike a Dog Rose in general appearance. The hybrids are briars too, most of them close to the wild in their general appearance, and therefore they will behave like wild briars, with long arching shoots, and no flowers after summer. Those least like the wild parent are 'Fritz Nobis' and 'Rosenwunder.' 'Fritz Nobis' is a beautiful flowering shrub, but not scented, an untypical member of the class.

Aside from these two recent examples, those listed at left were raised by Lord Penzance and introduced in 1894–1895.

RUGOSAS

'Scabrosa,' mauve red, single; 'Roseraie de l'Haÿ,' purple, double; 'Frau Dagmar Hartopp,' pink, single; R. rugosa alba, white, single; R. rugosa rubra, red, single; 'Pink Grootendorst,' pink, double, frilled; 'Vanguard,' orange salmon, double, practically a climber with very large flowers, summer only; 'Blanc Double de Coubert,'* white, double; 'Delicata,' pink, semi-double, rare; 'Fimbriata,' pink, double, frilled; 'Mrs. Anthony Waterer,' red, semi-double; 'Sarah van Fleet,' pink, semi-double.

Rosa rugosa, from which this class derives, is a wild rose from northeast China, Korea, and Japan. Its thick, deeply veined leaves are highly resistant to disease; it grows well in light soils and near the sea; the flowers are fairly large and appear over a long period, not in a short sharp burst; they are fragrant; the plants are shrubby, thick with leaves; the wood is pale in color, with many bristly prickles; the hips are large, red, and quick to ripen. These are excellent flowering shrubs and almost unbeatable as healthy hedges. Of the hybrids, those most nearly conforming to the foregoing specification are 'Frau Dagmar Hartopp,' *R. rugosa alba, R. rugosa rubra,* and 'Scabrosa'; and those most at variance are 'Conrad F. Meyer,' 'Mrs. Anthony Waterer,' 'Sarah van Fleet,' 'Schneezwerg,' and 'Vanguard.'

Much of the breeding has been by chance seedlings from Rugosa types, and the admixture of other roses has not as yet led so far as one might hope is possible.

Rose Gaujard

33 Sonia Meilland

34 Sutter's Gold

35 Super Star

36 Silver Jubilee

37 Wendy Cussons

38 Violinista Costa

39 Allgold

40 Taifun

53

41 Anne Harkness

Anne Cocker 42

44 Europeana

45 Escapade

Circus 46

47 Frensham

Margaret Merril 49

50   Lilli Marlene

51   Friesia

52 Prominent

53 Pink Parfait

Queen Elizabeth 54

56 Saga

58   Rob Roy

59 Stargazer

60 Sarabande

61 Southampton

32

ROSE GAUJARD

Hybrid Tea

A kind of silvery pink, very easy to grow, and free with its flowers. Closely inspected, it proves a bicolor, pink on the inner petal surface and white on the outer; but the white invades the inside, and the pink touches the outside, and the tips of the petals blush carmine, all making a precise account most difficult.

To the purists, 'Rose Gaujard' commits the sin of not wrapping its petals cleanly around its center, so that it opens with the heart of the flower cleft. The rose grower's term for that is a "split center." Raised in France by Jean Gaujard from 'Peace' × Seedling, this rose was introduced there in 1957, and in America by Armstrong Nurseries in 1964. Its plant qualities rather than its color and form gained its international reputation.

Those qualities are shown in the long life of the bush, and in the great many blooms it produces.

33

SONIA MEILLAND
syn SWEET PROMISE

Hybrid Tea

This famous rose is to be found in nearly every flower shop in the world; it is pink, with a lively touch of salmon orange to it. The flowers are fairly slim, the petals firmly entwined to make a bulbous base, to stretch modestly back and give the cone of the center a perfect position in the limelight. There are about 28 petals.

In places where the temperature is comfortable and people do not often shiver, 'Sonia Meilland' is a good garden rose, with the advantage of giving flowers to cut as good as the florists can sell. In cold places it is not at home.

It was raised in France by Alain Meilland from 'Zambra' × Seedling and introduced about 1973. Most of the people in the world's flower markets know it familiarly by the one word: 'Sonia.' 'Sweet Promise' is the British name.

Several sports, either lighter or darker in color, are now being grown.

34

SUTTER'S GOLD

Hybrid Tea

Beautiful ruddy gold buds open to yellow flowers, flushed with red. The keynote is elegance, to be seen in the smooth stems and dark leaves (they look fresh from the laundry); also in the bright sparkling flowers, breathing out a clean, sweet scent.

The first flowering of the season is usually the best, earlier than, and superior to, nearly all Hybrid Teas; it is never so good the rest of the summer. The flowers open rather quickly, having about 27 petals which readily part from one another; and the yellow steadily lightens from bud to petal fall.

'Sutter's Gold' was raised in California by Herbert Swim from 'Charlotte Armstrong' × 'Signora' and introduced by Armstrong Nurseries in 1950. It has been freely grown and greatly appreciated all over the rose-growing world.

It was named on the centenary of gold being struck in Sutter Creek, California.

35

SUPER STAR
syn TROPICANA

Hybrid Tea

One of the most famous of modern roses, because its color came as a revelation: not vermilion as often said, but rather a lustrous coral orange, well to the pink side of vermilion. The flowers are beautifully formed, having 30 petals almost perfectly disposed between the pointed center and reflexing surround. 'Super Star' is free-flowering, slightly taller than average, and moderately fragrant. It is likely to suffer from mildew.

It was raised in Germany by Mathias Tantau from two unnamed seedlings and introduced in 1960. Wherever it went, it was received with acclaim, and showered with awards. No other rose introduced in the 1960s achieved one-half the reputation of 'Super Star.' Jackson and Perkins introduced it in the United States as 'Tropicana.'

Liability to mildew is now a threat to this wonderful rose, and some nurserymen are already dropping it.

36

SILVER JUBILEE

Hybrid Tea

A long and silky flower, which is a regular confection of pink peaches and cream, very beautiful, elongated. The plants grow into compact mounds of leaves, dense, short, prolific in producing flowers, not even waiting for the stems to grow long.

The flowers have about 27 petals, and they hold them fairly close to a beautifully pointed heart for quite a while. Then they open rather suddenly, begin to fade, but shatter before old age can fulfill its threat of ugliness. There is a little scent.

This remarkable, sensational rose was raised from Seedling × 'Mischief' in Scotland by Alex Cocker, introduced in 1978, and was almost immediately in demand all round the world. The breeder himself died late in 1977, before the world had met his great creation.

The breeder took into his strain a rose bred from *R. kordesii;* thus 'Silver Jubilee's' different look.

37

WENDY CUSSONS

Hybrid Tea

A handsome bush with deep green, leathery leaves; a rose to plant in the expectation it will be no trouble to grow and will enjoy a long life. The flowers are rose red, highly fragrant, and well formed. It is one of the most free-flowering in its class.

The buds are almost scarlet, opening into rose-red flowers of about 30 petals, and finishing on the pink side of the borderline between red and pink. It looks fresh and pleasing at each stage.

Walter Gregory raised this good rose in England and introduced it in 1959. It was brought out in the United States in 1963 by Ilgenfritz Nurseries of Monroe, Michigan. The parents were not certainly known, but thought to be 'Independence' × 'Eden Rose.' It was enthusiastically received, especially in Britain, Holland, and the United States.

Its petals are among the best for making a somewhat scented rose wine.

38

VIOLINISTA COSTA

Hybrid Tea

A color as bright as a new fashion, and lively as new paint; for all that newness, it is quite an old rose.

The flowers have low centers; about 27 petals open flat, which is the best way to show the colors, for the brick red of the buds opens to a pink upper petal, cherry at the top, coral at the heart, very often with a suggestion of a white rim. Such flowers are profuse, upon bushes a little shorter than normal, garnished with holly-colored leaves.

Spain produced this rose, by the hands of Carlos Camprubi, from 'Sensation' × 'Shot Silk.' Introduced in 1936, it is now becoming neglected, except by a legion of old lovers.

It is a good example of a spreading bush.

39

ALLGOLD

Floribunda

This brilliant golden Floribunda seems to have all the virtues: a plant which sparkles in shiny dark leaf as well as in flower; a color which holds fast in excellent style; flowers that, although borne in clusters, and necessarily rather small, have a pretty shape and 20 petals to make it from; a dash of fragrance; and a compact, rather short habit of growth.

In short, a very good rose indeed, except in the hotter countries; it will only disappoint the person who expects his roses to grow big and fast.

It was raised in England by Edward Le Grice from 'Goldilocks' × 'Ellinor Le Grice,' and introduced in 1956. It is still grown pretty well all round the world, the puzzle being why was the American rating only fair?

Breeders find it most difficult to raise yellow roses of a pure color, held without fading. This was a fine shot at that goal.

40

TAIFUN syn TYPHOON

Hybrid Tea

One of the old-time favorites was 'Shot Silk,' and this may be taken as its modern counterpart, pink with orange and salmon shading, a yellow base, and a sweet scent. Where 'Shot Silk' was a light flower against grass-green leaves, this is a full one against foliage of a grayer cast. The 35 petals form a fine large flower, of particularly fine texture and handsome form.

The bushes grow strongly, rather more open than upright; and usually less than average height.

'Taifun' was raised by Reimer Kordes in Germany from 'Königin der Rosen' × 'Dr. A. J. Verhage,' and introduced in 1972; it is finding international favor somewhat slowly, but on firm recommendations from Germany and Britain. A rose of "shot" or mixed color is usually slow to find acceptance. The first choice in the public mind is almost always for a rose of one color, preferably red, secondly yellow or pink.

41

ANNE HARKNESS
syn HARKARAMEL

Floribunda

An individual rose, unusual in its long shoots, unusually beautiful in color and shape. The flowers are fairly small and double, charming in form, and of an amber yellow color sufficiently rare in roses to command admiration. They are borne in large clusters on tall shoots, which are so fine and slender, one would suppose the heads of the blooms were certain to weigh them down. By some mystery of mechanics, the shoots sway serenely, and it takes a fairly vicious storm to pull them down. There is only a little scent.

Owing to the length of shoot made beforehand, the flowers are later than most to appear; which means that 'Anne Harkness' is looking bright and fresh when most roses are finishing their first flush. Raised by the author from two unnamed seedlings, 'Anne Harkness' is to be introduced in 1980. It is therefore very much a rose of the future.

42

ANNE COCKER

Floribunda

The flowers are about the size of an overcoat button, only thicker, with 36 petals, most of which are expanded flat around a small cone in the center. The color is vermilion, very bright, and when the flowers are borne in one of the larger clusters, there may be dozens of them in it. They last a long time in water.

The plants are thorny, above average height, and at the end of their career the flowers lose their color and turn pale. The variety is later than most in flowering.

It was raised in Scotland by Alexander Cocker from 'Highlight' × 'Königin der Rosen,' and introduced in 1971. It is grown in many countries, being especially liked by showmen.

For them its durability after being cut is a great advantage. One flower arranger, with skillful care, used the same flowers for over a week, in three different countries.

43

ARTHUR BELL

Floribunda

A vigorous plant, on which we find golden yellow flowers of pleasantly wide structure in perfect harmony with the smart green leaves.

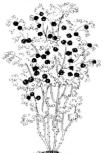

The growth is taller than average, and sometimes becomes leggy. The clusters are usually of a few flowers. The flowers open their 19 petals into a bowl shape, then flatten out, losing their yellow at this stage, so that the bush carries both yellow and white blooms. The yellow lasts better out of the full sun; and 'Arthur Bell' is a very good autumn rose. Sam McGredy raised this rose in Northern Ireland from 'Cläre Grammerstorf' × 'Piccadilly,' and introduced it in 1965.

44

EUROPEANA

Floribunda

Red in leaf and bloom, the young leaves purple, the flowers shining and dark, as red as anyone could wish. They are so full of petals that to count would be misleading, for many small petals go to make the charming rosette shape. The flowers are borne in large clusters. For many districts, this is easily the finest dark red Floribunda; but it is spoiled in some areas by mildew, especially if the plants do not regularly receive their requirement of water. The growth is bushy, normally covered with foliage and flowers down to the ground. Little scent. 'Europeana' was raised in Holland by Gijsbert de Ruiter from 'Ruth Leuwerik' × 'Rosemary Rose'; he introduced it in 1963, and the Conard-Pyle Company did so in America in 1968. It is rated excellent in the United States and is grown all over the world, perhaps most in northern Europe.

45

ESCAPADE

Floribunda

This most unusual rose can best be appreciated when the flowers are expanded in the sun; they are rosy violet and white, the centers all white except for the yellow stamens and stigmas. There are about 12 petals, opening into flat and wide flowers, pleasantly scented. It is a most effective rose in a vase, quite a surprise to anyone who does not know it. The clusters contain many flowers; the plants are bushy, above average height, and the foliage is light green. 'Escapade' was raised by the author in England from 'Pink Parfait' × 'Baby Faurax'; it was introduced in 1967 and welcomed with much enthusiasm, particularly in European countries. The enthusiasm was from the experts and the showmen, who saw it as something different from existing roses; it is recommended in Germany as one of the most suitable roses to mix with other plants.

46

CIRCUS

Floribunda

One of the great favorites in the 1950s and 1960s, when the vogue for Floribundas with neat double flowers was at its height. The trend today is toward larger flowers. The charm of 'Circus' is its color and shape; the flowers are orange yellow, with red on the outer petals; the red is shaded into the flower in varying degrees. It looks as smart as any painted lady, with every little petal in place, around a short but elegant heart. Short, bushy growth. There are other strains of 'Circus,' of which the pale one is coarse in growth and unattractive in color; the deeper one is a fine orange red color, and is sold in America as 'Circus Parade,' and in Britain as 'Alison Wheatcroft,' the American being more double. Many nurseries have ceased to grow 'Circus' because of its tendency to change to the pale strain; more's the pity. 'Circus' was raised in California by Herbert Swim and introduced in 1956.

47

FRENSHAM

Floribunda

A large and prickly shrub, with cheerful red flowers and shiny leaves. It flowers very freely in large clusters, the dark red flowers opening from well-formed buds to semi-double. They have about 15 petals.

In places where this will grow without too much trouble from mildew, it is one of the most handsome of roses as a shrub or hedge. Although normally considered a Floribunda, it is about twice as tall and wide as the average. There is hardly any scent.

It is one of the few of the world's favorite roses to have been raised by an amateur; he was Albert Norman, by trade a jewel cutter in London. His rose was introduced in 1946 and became a worldwide success. The parents were Seedling × 'Crimson Glory.'

There is no need to remove the old flowers from 'Frensham,' because it makes no seed pods. Should anyone find seed on it, then it ought to be sown.

48

MARLENA

Floribunda

A short and compact red Floribunda, very popular in accordance with a modern interest in short growing plants for small gardens and patios. The dark red color satisfies the eye, being bright as well as dark, and agreeing well with the bronze tints in the small leaves. It is really a splendid little plant.

The flowers are semi-double, well formed of about 18 petals, many of them set close in the small clusters. It should be planted closer together than normal Floribundas, if one wants to conceal the ground between the plants. 'Marlena' was raised by Reimer Kordes in Germany from 'Gertrud Westphal' × 'Lilli Marlene' and introduced in 1964. Jackson and Perkins introduced it in the United States in 1967.

Sometimes after the first flush, 'Marlena' makes many twiggy shoots, and looks a muddle. It should be trimmed well back after its summer flowering.

49

MARGARET MERRIL

Floribunda

Here is fragrance sweeter than any rose, a rare delight. It is breathed from waxy white flowers, with a touch of blush about them, formed of 28 petals into the shape of a Hybrid Tea of perfect high pointed center, but smaller.

The bushes grow vigorously, with handsome leaves; the flowers grow in clusters of a few blooms each, which means that the plants are not profusely covered with them. 'Margaret Merril' is perhaps the only Floribunda in which the quality of the individual bloom is of more importance than the massed effect.

It was raised by the author in England from Seedling × 'Pascali' and introduced in 1977, immediately being received with enthusiasm, especially in Britain, Switzerland, and Italy.

The seedling used was bred from the Kordes pink Floribunda 'Rudolph Timm'; and that was bred by Kordes from a Sweet Briar; a valuable line.

50

LILLI MARLENE

Floribunda

A favorite bedding rose, because planting it is like unwinding a crimson carpet over the ground, so prolific and colorful is 'Lilli Marlene.' The flowers have about 25 petals, are of medium size, and set close together in the clusters. Their scarlet tones are seen as the petals unfold from dark buds, but the general color effect is of a brilliant deep red. The plants are bushy, compact, a little below average height. There is not very much fragrance; and possibly the variety is rather more efficient than elegant in the eyes of the aesthetic.

'Lilli Marlene' was raised in Germany by Reimer Kordes from Seedling × 'Ama' and introduced in 1959. Since then it has been grown all round the world. There are other red Floribundas more attractive in flower form and in leaf than this one. But 'Lilli Marlene' holds hers close together, dense where other Floribundas tend to be sparser.

51

FRIESIA
syn KORRESIA, SUNSPRITE

Floribunda

This golden yellow Floribunda has larger flowers than 'Allgold,' of a most attractive, well-filled form. The plants are compact, slightly less than average height; the leaves are glossy, grassy green. The color effect is all the more vivid because the flowers are so large and full; thus each presents a fine area of gold. Pleasantly scented.

'Korresia' tends to bloom on the top of the plant, not so much at the sides. It is likely to lose wood to the frost.

Raised by Reimer Kordes in Germany from 'Friedrich Wörlein' × 'Spanish Sun' and introduced in 1973, it is already a leading variety in many countries. 'Korresia' is the name used in Britain; but Continental Europe, Australia, and New Zealand call it 'Friesia'; and in the United States it is 'Sunsprite.'

'Allgold' in its long reign has seen no greater challenger than this.

52

PROMINENT syn KORP

Floribunda

Bright vermilion; it looks as if the color was laid on thick, to test if the eye could be affronted by a surfeit; and the flowers shine defiantly, as if guilty at being so gaudy. They are well formed in the bud, like small Hybrid Teas of about 45 petals; indeed this rose is halfway to being a Hybrid Tea. The blooms are just right for a buttonhole.

Several blooms are carried on a stem, and when fully open they show a split center. The foliage is full and light, not too well in accord with the vermilion flowers. This rose has little scent.

'Prominent' was raised in Germany by Reimer Kordes from 'Königin der Rosen' × 'Zorina,' and introduced in 1970.

It is one of a number of similar roses, raised with an eye to the flower shops. The most successful florist's rose from Herr Kordes in this color is 'Mercedes,' distinguished by a slight twist in its heart.

53

PINK PARFAIT

Floribunda

Pink no doubt it is, a very dainty color too, as if painted onto the creamy petal. Sometimes the painting is incomplete, and the creaminess shares the flower with the pink. In either case it is beautiful, a long flower for a Floribunda, with a sweet straight center, and about 22 petals to the bloom.

The growth is bushy, a little shorter than average. The plants are not very thorny, and they flower with great freedom. If the petals do not fall when they are old, they start to die in an ugly way. Wind normally removes them. There is not much scent.

This rose was raised in California by Herbert Swim from 'First Love' × 'Pinocchio' and introduced by Armstrong Nurseries in 1960. It has been rated an excellent rose just about everywhere.

Many Floribundas make excellent cut flowers; this is one of the best. A single stem can be enough for a vase, given a good cluster.

54

QUEEN ELIZABETH

Floribunda

In America this rose is classed as a Grandiflora; it does not easily fit any class, because it stands on its own, a tall plant lifting clusters of lovely pink roses up to the sky. The leaves are broad and dark, the bush upright, vigorous, handsome, outgrowing most others. It is certainly one of the great successes of twentieth-century roses; many people would say the greatest.

The flowers are light but colorful pink, with random flushes of carmine on the outer petals. They are of moderate size (which makes nonsense of the term Grandiflora), very well formed as pointed buds, eventually opening wide. They have about 35 petals; not much scent. They are good for cutting.

Dr. Walter E. Lammerts raised this royal champion in California from 'Charlotte Armstrong' × 'Floradora.' It was introduced by Germain's Nursery of Los Angeles in 1954.

55

PRINCESS CHICHIBU

Floribunda

A beautifully formed Floribunda, one of the best to cut. The heart of the flower is much lighter than its surrounding petals, a happy contrast of light pink with a touch of orange, and rose red robes around it. The form is like that of a compact 'Pink Parfait,' but with more petals.

The plants grow medium height or rather less, bushy, compact, with plenty of dark leaves.

This variety received its name to honor a Japanese princess and is grown in that country. It has also done well in other countries, especially in Germany; but it never caught on in Britain, possibly for the reason that it suffers some discoloration as the flowers reach the end of their days. Up to that time, from bud to full bloom, it is fresh and sparkling.

It was introduced in 1971, having been raised by the author from seedling × 'Merlin'; the latter was a somewhat similar rose.

56

SAGA

Floribunda

This is a shrubby Floribunda, for although it is not much taller than normal, it does grow wider, to form a pleasant, rounded bush.

The attractive leaves are deep green, with a slight twist in them.

The flowers are ivory, semi-double, with a pleasing form, perhaps because they look slightly ruffled. They have one great virtue: they appear early and continue through the season without any lengthy intermission. 'Saga' has a little scent.

'Saga' can make a very pleasant hedge, or stand as a shrub in its own right. It was raised by the author and introduced in 1974. The parents were 'Rudolph Timm' × seedling.

'Saga' is not easily fitted into modern rose planting schemes. In the old days, it would have been promptly called a Hybrid Musk, and would have shared a niche with those popular shrub roses. In another chapter we suggest some new planting schemes.

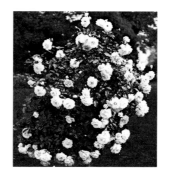

57

SCHNEEWITTCHEN
syn ICEBERG

Floribunda

Masses upon masses of small white flowers glisten upon this plant, as if they would never tire of tilting their little hearts toward our eyes; and then they expand as wide as they are able, which is farther than one would expect.

The plant is best seen with space to grow, not crammed into a bed, because it is a fine round plant, flowering all round the sides as well as on top. It can be a handsome shrub, and is one of the best to use as a Standard, or Tree Rose. Sometimes the flowers have a flush of pink. It has a little scent, which can become pleasant since so many blooms contribute to it.

This fine rose comes from Germany, where Reimer Kordes raised it from 'Robin Hood' × 'Virgo.' It was introduced in 1958. The French call it 'Fée des Neiges.'

Some blackspot problems; but it is far too dainty to receive so menacing and solid a name as 'Iceberg.'

58

ROB ROY

Floribunda

Dark, glowing red, the crimson of it gleaming with scarlet lights, most rich and beautiful. The flowers are large for a Floribunda, with about 22 petals. As buds, they are perfect buttonholes; on the plant, they open into wide blooms, holding red to the end.

This excellent Floribunda is one of the best to give a long succession of high-quality blooms. For all its loveliness, it is not at first sight a mass of color in the normal Floribunda manner; it seems to prefer continuity, spacing its flowers rather wide in the clusters. There is not much scent.

'Rob Roy' was raised in Scotland by Alexander Cocker and introduced in 1971. The parents were 'Evelyn Fison' × 'Wendy Cussons.'

There is some susceptibility to blackspot; but in that case a gardener with a glasshouse can enjoy its beauty to the full, for blackspot is not usually to be seen under glass.

59

STARGAZER

Floribunda

This low growing rose is studded with single flowers of five petals, so close together as to hide the bush entirely. They are orange red, with a yellow eye at the center, marked in the form of a star; hence, of course, the name; it is the beholder, not the rose, who is the 'Stargazer.' The color loses its brightness as the flowers age; but if trimmed off, the old blooms will soon be replaced by new ones. And the sense of dazzling abundance remains. Although one rarely thinks of cutting single (five-petaled) roses for a vase, it is worth trying the experiment with 'Stargazer.' It makes a lovely low arrangement; it has to be low, because the bushes, and therefore the stems, are short. The leaves are mat; they would be better if deeper in color or glossy. 'Stargazer' was raised in England by the author from 'Marlena' × 'Kim' and it was introduced in 1977.

60

SARABANDE

Floribunda

This spreading bush keeps below average height, and proceeds to cram into its allotted space so many red flowers that it might seem a miracle. They have about nine petals each and are fairly wide, certainly not babies. The color is scarlet, slightly geranium red. It can be a wonderful sight, very suitable to grow at the edge of a path or border. The center begins to pale with age, but the petals fall quickly before any further deterioration occurs. There is hardly any scent. Raised in France by Francis Meilland from 'Cocorico' × 'Moulin Rouge,' this rose was introduced in 1957. It is really so marvelously good, that a loud protest ought to echo around the rose world, to discourage those nurserymen who discard it on the grounds that people can be persuaded to buy double roses only. Unfortunately there is some truth in their fears, but 'Sarabande' could easily overturn them.

61

SOUTHAMPTON

Floribunda

Apricot flushed red; somebody likened it to marmalade, and because it is unusually healthy for a rose in that color group, it is becoming popular. The flowers have about 26 petals; they start as nicely pointed buds and finish wide open, the central petals incurved. 'Southampton' tolerates extremes of summer weather well, whether rain or hot sun. The growth is vigorous and upright, rather above average height; the leaves are dark, abundant, rather small. It has a pleasant scent, not strong. A bed or hedge of 'Southampton' is a splendid sight in full flower, and it varies its brand of marmalade according to the season's weather. It was raised in England by the author from Seedling × 'Yellow Cushion' and introduced in 1972. 'Susan Ann' is its Swiss name. For planting in parks, it is almost ideal, thanks to its vigor, bright color, and robust health.

ENJOYING YOUR ROSES

The crowning glory of a rose garden: a good climber trained on a trellis. 'Albertine,' a Wichuraiana Hybrid, bears unusually rich, full blooms that seem to defy gravity.

The two aspects of enjoying roses are growing them for the pleasure of seeing their beauty, and doing things with them when they are grown.

Whether one has a huge garden in which hundreds of roses can be planted, or a tiny plot big enough for only three, the enjoyment can be equal. In fact, the owner of a small plot has this great advantage over his more expansive brother: he can make it more perfect, because his attention per square meter is at a higher ratio.

Even the city dweller without a garden, whose roses all come from the florist shop, can find much pleasure in the arrangement and display of cut-flower roses (see below).

We begin by surveying the gardening possibilities using single plants, or clumps, and the chapter continues with combinations in beds, hedges, borders, cover plants, and finally arranging and propagation.

This chapter offers a variety of suggestions for landscaping and arranging. For technical advice on the actual planting and cultivation of roses, the reader is addressed to the chapter beginning on page 145.

SINGLE PLANTS OR CLUMPS

Practically any rose may be grown in isolation, either just one plant of it, or else a group, after the fashion in which any other flowering shrubs are grown. The result of planting a group of more than one plant of the same variety is to make the clump look like an enormous single plant; and the

In deciding between clumps, beds, borders, and the like, the gardener must keep the overall scheme in mind. This garden shows an oval bed in the foreground, with a border (which includes Tree roses) behind. With less space, a clump of three to five plants, or even a single bush, could be used instead of the oval bed.

Opposite: *Spectacular effects can be achieved with climbers, space permitting. The large, plentiful rose-red blooms of 'Ritter von Barmstede' have transformed one corner of the Regent's Park, in London, into a bower. (See the discussion of "Cover Plants," which includes information on frames, page 81.)*

size and shape of it should be chosen to agree with its surroundings. What is sufficient in a small garden may look insignificant in a large one; and what is impressive in a large garden may unhappily crowd a small one. Clumps of three can be planted in a triangle; of five, in an egg-shape.

This is a pleasing way to grow roses, for it accords with their natural habit of growing in colonies in the wild. There is also the prospect of greater resistance to disease, because free-standing plants are dried after rain better than those closely planted in a bed; and some diseases enjoy humid conditions.

In choosing varieties, one should consider what height and lateral spread are most desirable. These are the first two points, because the plant (or clump) has to be part of the garden's architecture. The third point should be foliage, that it be both handsome and healthy. The color of the flowers therefore comes fourth, although most people put it first. It should not automatically be assumed that red is the best color. Creamy yellow, soft pink, and even white can be as spectacular as red.

Out of the enormous range of roses suitable for growing in isolation, whether singly or in clumps, the following are suggested in order of preference:

SHORT. 'Cécile Brunner'; 'Frau Dagmar Hartopp'; 'Sarabande'; 'National Trust'; 'The Fairy.' *Planting distance in clumps, 60–80 cm (24–32 in.).*

MEDIUM. 'Schneewittchen syn Iceberg'; 'Golden Wings'; 'Ophelia'; 'Pascali'; 'Michèle Meilland.' *Planting distance in clumps, 80–100 cm (32–39 in.).*

TALL UPRIGHT. 'Alexander'; 'Queen Elizabeth'; 'Southampton'; 'Pink Favorite'; R. rubrifolia; *a climber, rambler, or trailer tied to an upright post. Planting distance in clumps, 80–100 cm (32–39 in.).*

TALL SPREADING. 'Fritz Nobis'; 'Canary Bird'; 'Golden Chersonese'; 'Scabrosa'; R. virginiana. *Planting distance in clumps, 1½–2 meters (5–6½ ft).*

VERY LARGE. 'Geranium'; 'New Dawn'; 'Marguerite Hilling'; 'Frühlingsgold'; R. spinosissima hispida; *climbers, provided with stout posts about 1½ meters out of the ground to which to support the lower part of the shoots. Planting distance in clumps, 2 meters.*

BEDS

The most popular way of growing roses is in a bed; which is to say a small area marked off from its surroundings, and totally filled with roses. Bedding was popular long before roses were thought suitable for it. The focal parts of the garden were selected and prepared for plants such as tulips, geraniums, calceolarias, or dahlias. Sometimes they were changed two or three times in a season, to provide a succession of bloom. When the rose developed to its present state of bountiful blooming twice or thrice in the same season, it was seen as a more durable, more beautiful, and cheaper substitute for the previously favored bedding plants. In Aberdeen the Director of Parks states that roses are cheaper than grass to maintain.

Many types of roses can be grown in a bed, but the most spectacular are Floribundas and Hybrid Teas. The highest expression of abundance is undoubtedly provided by using one variety to a bed. This is well enough in a large garden, where plenty of beds can be made; but it is painful to the owner of a small garden, who wishes to grow and know more varieties. In that case, he must choose between his two desires, remembering that he can do as he likes in his own garden, but that the spectacle of abundance may diminish in ratio to the number of varieties he mixes together.

The distance between plants may vary according to the size of the variety chosen, and according to the luxuriance of growth expected in one's climate; but these factors are normally included in the range of 40–100 cm (16–39 in.). Thus a compact variety in a frosty climate can be planted 40 cm (16 in.) apart, an average variety about 60 cm (24 in.), and a vigorous variety about 80 cm (32 in.). If little or no frost damage is expected, then the measurements can increase about 20 cm (8 in.) each.

A bed can be agreeably augmented by planting one or more Standard (Tree) roses, preferably of a height that will ensure that the stem of the Standard is hidden by the bushes when they are mature. If the Standard and the bushes are of the same variety, so much the better.

Beds can be of any size and any shape; they are part of the furniture of the garden and need to be correct in proportion and contour. The owner's good taste must settle those points; there is no universal recipe, any more than for the furniture of a room. But it may be noted that an isolated square or rectangle has a good chance of being wrong; that a bed too wide to be cultivated from the edges is more

A short list of some of the best roses, in order of preference, to provide splendid beds; there are of course many more.

'National Trust,' red
'Southampton,' apricot orange
'Schneewittchen syn Iceberg,' white
'Sarabande,' scarlet
'Pink Parfait,' creamy pink
'Alexander,' vermilion, tall
'Sutter's Gold,' yellow and pink
'Lilli Marlene,' crimson
'Friesia syn Korresia,' yellow
'Blessings,' pink
'John Waterer,' crimson
'Elizabeth Harkness,' ivory
'Piccadilly,' red and yellow
'Chicago Peace,' pink and yellow
'Wendy Cussons,' pink
'Pascali,' white
'Rob Roy,' crimson
'Allgold,' yellow
'Escapade,' rosy violet
'Michèle Meilland,' light pink

Right: *When the proper planting distances are observed, a bed of roses will grow to form a whole, with the undergrowth lost from view. Here we see part of an effective bed of 'Masquerade' (a Floribunda).*

difficult to maintain; and that if the bed is in grass, it should be of a suitable shape to be circumnavigated by the lawn mower. The bed should be in sympathy with the other lines and shapes created by plants in the garden.

Beds may be associated in an overall design. This was once a common pattern of a rose garden, but is less fashionable now, partly because of the work entailed in edging and tidying; partly because taste has veered away from formality.

The method of marking out beds for planting is explained under "Planting" in the chapter "How to Grow Roses." It is not necessary to put the plants in files, although if the shape of the bed allows it, then files are easier for hoeing. Many people prefer a less formal, that is, a more staggered manner of planting. In fact, once the plants have grown, the positions are usually hidden under the canopy of foliage.

It is possible to make beds of roses other than Floribundas and Hybrid Teas. Even climbers and trailers can be grown handsomely in a round bed, by providing a very stout post at the center, with wires or other connections into ring bolts driven in at the perimeter. Plant about $1\frac{1}{2}$ to 2 meters (5 to $6\frac{1}{2}$ ft) apart.

Most rosarians dislike planting other flowers in rose beds, for the good reasons that the roses will probably smother them, and rose roots are not to be disturbed by digging. Probably the owner of a large garden will be satisfied with this advice. But the small plot is different; every space becomes filled, and the spaces between roses will contain such plants as violas, saxifrages, petunias.

An unusual combination: with climbers covering the wall, behind a foreground of other roses. This type of arrangement, in which a bed is combined with a tall background, is called a border. (Borders are discussed in detail on page 80.)

Above left: 'Manning's Blush,' a Sweet Briar hybrid of the eighteenth century, forming a graceful specimen plant.

HEDGES

Roses can provide nearly every kind of hedge a gardener can require, except a tall narrow one. Anyone who wants a squared-off hedge kept firmly in place had better forget roses. They are plants of a soft, hazy outline, ideal for the gardener who wishes to throw away his hedging shears.

Roses recommended for hedges:

SHORT COMPACT. 'National Trust'; 'Sarabande'; 'The Fairy'; 'Landora syn Sunblest'; 'Wendy Cussons'; 'Pink Favorite.'

TALLER, BUSHIER. 'Schneewittchen syn Iceberg'; 'Southampton'; 'Golden Wings'; 'Ballerina' (or 'Mozart'); 'Escapade'; 'Frensham'; 'Penelope'; 'Yesterday.'

TALLER, UPRIGHT. 'Alexander'; 'Queen Elizabeth.'

TALL AND WIDE. As mentioned in text.

Why they are not planted almost universally as hedges is hard to understand.

A hedge is a line of plants along a boundary. The boundary is not necessarily at the edge of the property; for interior boundaries can mark interior limits, just as both houses and rooms have walls as their boundaries.

The main factors governing selection are height, width, health, and leafy bases. It is important to keep width in mind, because many types of roses spread out farther than one realizes at planting time. The planting line must be determined with due thought to the likely lateral encroachment in future.

Most people, therefore, will be bound to choose roses of fairly upright growth. But if space permits it, the most wonderful rose hedges can be made from some of the larger shrubs in the genus.

Hedges may be planted in one or more rows, according to

the width the owner desires. A short hedge is usually best made by using one variety; a longer hedge may be of mixed varieties at the owner's pleasure.

The most delightful of all rose hedges, granted that space is no problem, can be made out of two rows, a meter (a yard) apart, of such roses as 'Cornelia,' 'Golden Chersonese,' 'Fritz Nobis,' 'Scabrosa,' 'Souvenir de la Malmaison,' 'Frühlings-gold,' *R. farreri persetosa,* 'Nevada,' 'Celestial' (and other

Albas), 'Golden Wings,' 'Roseraie de l'Haÿ,' 'New Dawn,' 'Geranium,' 'Canary Bird,' 'Marguerite Hilling,' *R. spinosis-sima hispida,* and *R. virginiana.* Plant them in fives (three back row, two front row; and the next variety two back row, three front row, etc.). The order in which they are shown would do very well. Such a hedge will average 2 meters (6 ft) in height, about 4 meters (12 ft) wide; and it will provide so much difference of character from spring to winter, as to interest and delight its owner.

For those with less spacious premises, a short list of hedge roses is given in the box on the opposite page, in order of preference; the planting distances are approximately 55 cm (22 in.) for the short ones, and as much as 75 cm (30 in.) for the taller.

An alternative is to train climbers or trailers along a prepared structure, such as may be made from posts and rails, prefer-ably with a taller post at intervals.

Above left: *A hedge made up en-tirely of one rose variety. This is about as regular and smooth a shape as rose hedges can assume.*

Left: *'Sarabande' is appropriate for short, compact hedges.*

The hedge shown above consists of several different rose varieties brought together. If space allows, two rows can be planted together for a thick hedge.

A border is a bed with a background such as a wall, fence, hedge, or other plants. It usually runs alongside some feature, such as a lawn or terrace; consequently its normal shape is long and narrow. It may be the only strip of soil in a tiny front garden, close to a wall; in this case roses of rounded

1 'Geranium' (1)
2 'Queen Elizabeth' (3)
3 'Canary Bird' (1)
4 'Alexander' (3)
5 R. rubrifolia (3)
6 'Crimson Shower'
   (on post) (1)
7 'Golden Chersonese' (1)
8 'Pascali' (3)
9 'Southampton' (3)
10 'Peace' (3)
11 'Joseph's Coat' (3)
12 'Golden Wings' (3)
13 'Schneewittchen' (3)
14 'Frau Dagmar Hartopp' (5)

15 'Allgold' (5)
16 'National Trust' (5)
17 'The Fairy' (5)
18 'Silver Jubilee' (5)
19 R. chinensis viridiflora (5)
20 'John Waterer' (5)
21 'Sutter's Gold' (5)
22 'Yesterday' (5)

habit should be chosen in preference to upright ones. It may be a lordly array, accentuating some vista in a great estate. Borders may be composed of any kinds of plants mixed together. Roses are particularly valuable in that case, because they flower when many perennials and shrubs have finished. But one must choose the varieties with an eye to their agreeing with their neighbors, at least to one's own taste. It can be argued that Hybrid Teas and double Floribundas look too sophisticated; and that single or semi-double roses fit in more naturally.

Borders can also be made of roses alone; the old idea of a herbaceous border has not been stolen by rosarians as it could be. The genus contains sufficient variations of height, habit, color, character, and flowering times to make the idea perfectly attractive. Taking these points, consider the plan illustrated here for a method of rose growing which has been very little practiced, but which offers countless fascinating possibilities.

The figures in parentheses suggest the minimum number of plants needed to keep each part in relationship. Such a border could be planted in an area approximately 15 × 3.5 meters (49 × 11½ ft).

COVER PLANTS

Climbing or trailing roses can be used to cover various structures, with spectacular results. Two basic rules should be remembered: never leave long shoots untied, or else they are likely to be broken by the wind. Do not wait for pruning time, but rather tie them as soon as they are noticed. And

Climbing or trailing roses. of which there are some recent developments called "ground cover" roses. can be used to cover existing walls. fences. sheds. tree stumps: or structures can be built to support them. in the form of posts. tripods. arches. and pergolas. With structures such as shown here. a ball of string and some staples will solve the problems of attachment.

The arrangement shown below combines thick rope with wood supports. Both elements will be hidden. in time. beneath the thickening foliage.

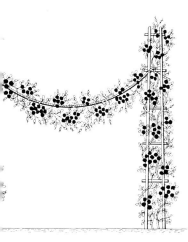

if the structure permits it, tie them as far as possible in lateral directions, for the plant will normally fill the upward direction with ease. A rough guide to the distance to leave between trained shoots on a wall is elbow to knuckles. "Ground cover" by roses is quite in the fashion; but the customers expected for such roses are municipalities rather than amateurs. Unless weeds are completely controlled while the plants are becoming established, the strong possibility is that the eventual ground cover will be weeds and not roses. Some roses naturally grow through trees, in order to bloom in great cascades once they have grown through the tree to the light. They can be planted under trees of between 8 and 16 meters (26–52 ft) in height. Do not place them against the trunk but away from it, under some of the lower overhanging branches. Leave them for two or three years to grow into a mound, like brambles; they may need some water in that period. Thereafter some long stems will arise and start climbing through the tree. They are more likely to flower on the side of the tree sheltered from the prevailing wind. Suitable roses for growing through trees are *R. filipes, R. helenae,* and *R. longicuspis.* Banksian roses may also be grown in this way.

Several examples of special supports for climbing roses are shown in the sketches on this page. The gardener should not forget that walls and fences can also be used: or simplest of all. one stout post.

CUTTING AND ARRANGING ROSES

The rose has a gentle simplicity about its beauty, which makes it the most heartwarming of all flowers in a vase in the house. It does not have a long life after being cut, but its life can be lengthened by some simple care.

The cool of the day is the best time to cut roses from the garden, and they should be placed in water at once. Roses bought from a florist should already have been in water, but they ought to be kept cool, out of the sun and wind, until they arrive home. Whether from garden or flower shop, once the roses are in the house one should remove the bottom leaves, cut off the base of the stem, scrape a sliver of bark from the bottom few centimeters (about an inch) of the stem, and replace the blooms in deep water. Let them spend several hours in a cool place, preferably dark, in that state. Materials are on sale to add to the water in order to prolong the life of flowers. In the absence of these, some sugar will help.

After being refreshed and replenished in deep water in a cool place, the roses may be arranged at one's pleasure. They will live longest in a cool and draft-free position.

It is not necessary to cut a great armful of roses to the detriment of both the bushes and the garden. A few flowers can look just as lovely as a crowded mass.

A pleasing arrangement imitates some shape, whether a circle, a triangle, a column, an arc, or some other homogeneous form. It does not have to follow the shape exactly, but only to suggest it.

An unpleasing arrangement usually fails by suggesting no shape; or by amalgamating two or more contradictory shapes; or by following a shape in too crowded or stiff a manner.

Roses at different stages look well together; for example, a bud at the top, and an expanded bloom at the base, can add grace to the arrangement.

Colors mix more easily than is usually thought, and so do types. If there is a choice of color, a good solid red is better at the base than at the top. White is better at the perimeter than at the center. Scarlet and lilac, against all expectation, magnify one another in proximity. Yellows should not be all together, but in a kind of chain, interrupted by the other colors.

These are matters of personal taste. Some people attain a high degree of artistry. Others pop a stem in a jam jar. As long as they both enjoy the result, they are equally right.

Arrangements in a vase can be very simple, very ornate, or anything in between. The combination of a bud and an open blossom offers an elegant and satisfying simplicity. The rule is to place the bud above and behind the flower. The photograph shows 'Sonia Meilland.'

BUTTONHOLES

The sooner this innocent habit is restored to general use, the better.

The requirements are a rose and a container. The container is a small tube with a pin or other fastening attached. Plastic tubes are cheap, clean, and virtually unbreakable.

Two types of rose can often combine in a pleasing arrangement. Here the clusters of small blooms set off the larger ones.

Above right: *Two artful examples of the effective combination of roses with other cut flowers: with irises (center). and with cottage pinks (or carnations). arranged in a teapot.*

The tube should be filled about four-fifths with water, and pinned to the garment in a vertical position. It is more easily done when the garment is hanging up.

The rose should be cut several hours before it is to be worn, on a short stem, and left in water in a cool place. It should be cut quite young, the outer petals just unfolding. Even though it is reduced to a very short stem, when placed in a buttonhole, it will stay fresh as a result of having spent several hours in water beforehand.

Buttonholes look best in the lapel of a jacket, with the container concealed behind, and the rose through the hole.

EXHIBITING

The ordinary gardener thinks that exhibitors are either show-offs or prize hunters.

That is not kind, nor is it correct, except in a minority of cases. Exhibitors may be slightly crazy; but they are notably amiable, and their world has a fascination that nobody should decry without testing it for himself. The flavor of a flower show is not that of ordinary life.

Anyone who wants to exhibit for the first time, just to sample the experience, should make personal contact with a more experienced exhibitor, who may be located by an enquiry to an officer of the organization that runs the show.

The illustrations indicate a few of the many possible containers that can be used for unusual effects with cut roses. Some containers, depending on their shape, will suggest special arrangements.

In this way he will obtain answers to his elementary questions, a support to lean on during the time of putting up the blooms, and the confidence to do it.

The new exhibitor will be wise to make his first attempt upon a modest scale, say one or two classes which only require a few blooms. He must submit his entry by the stipulated time, and remember that the schedule of classes means exactly what it says, in the most literal sense. For example, three blooms means three; not two or four, but exactly three. He will be wise to take at least twice as many, and some at different stages, in order to cover his inexperience; but he must only present three in a class for three.

The first essential is to take the flowers to the show in good condition. Cut them the day before, and treat them as recommended in the section on cutting and arranging roses. If it is possible, take them to the show in water, without letting the flowers be knocked or jostled together. But if they have to be carried dry, put them in water immediately upon arrival.

This basket-type vase allows for an eye-catching horizontal arrangement of 'Coral Cluster,' a Polyantha.

Left bottom: *White 'Pascali' set off against especially chosen foliage. Many diverse leaf types can be used with roses.*

ROSE HIP WINE

2 liters (quarts) rose hips
4 liters (quarts) water
1½ kg (3 lbs) white sugar
1 teaspoon yeast

Collect hips when first softened by frost. Wash and crush them thoroughly into a pulp, and put them into a jar. Make syrup with warmed water and sugar and pour onto hips, then add the yeast when the syrup is cool enough. Place in an air-tight container. Keep at a steady temperature, 15–20°C (60–70°F), until fermentation ceases. Strain carefully into a clean jar, and keep in a cold place for two weeks.* Siphon again into a fresh jar and keep it cold for six months in the cellar. Bottle, and store the bottles in a cool place on their sides for at least a further six months before tasting.
Never use metal utensils or containers in preparing your wines, and make certain all bottles, etc., are perfectly clean.

ROSE PETAL PRESERVES

½ kg (1 lb) rose petals
Water
1½ kg (3 lb) white sugar

Pick the petals when they are dry and half to full open, but not going over. Put them into a pan with sufficient water just to cover them, and boil until they are tender. It may take one or two hours; try biting one, it should be slightly firm when cooked. They will appear to lose their color, but the end product will be colorful. Add the sugar, one-third of it at a time, stirring each until it is dissolved. Boil gently until setting point is reached.

In some classes, the organization provides the vases; in others, the exhibitor; this will be clear from the schedule in any well-run show. In either case, leave the flowers in water while preparing the vase. The preparation consists of making the vase look clean, inserting something to hold the flowers straight (a bundle of rushes from the old hands, oasis by the up-to-date, and chunks of newspaper by the ill-prepared), and then filling the vase with water.

Now read the schedule again, to prevent any error, and then take all the flowers out of the container in one movement together, and lay them on the bench with their heads in a dry place. This is much better than picking them out one by one, and shaking the remainder each time.

Pick up the top one, and if it looks good, put it in the vase; if it is not one of the best, leave it aside. Just arrange them as best you can, leaving a more or less equal space between each bloom. When finished, check that the exhibit obeys the schedule; obtain and place whatever exhibitor's identification is provided by the organizers, and leave the flowers in peace to astonish the judges.

Next time, the new exhibitor will know twenty times as much, just from the taste of his first experience.

It is fun to increase plants; and although at first sight it appears much cheaper than buying them, that is only because the gardener does not pay for his own time. If he did, they would be ten times more expensive.

Amateur propagators often fall into the trap of supposing

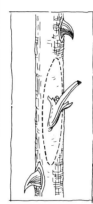
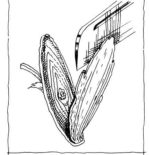

Budding, as done for commercial propagation, is carried out in the six steps shown here. (1) A T-shaped cut is made into the stock of a wild rose plant. (2) An eye is cut off the rose that is to be propagated, in an oval shape. (3) The layer of wood is removed from the back of the eye with a knife. (4) The eye is slid into the T-cut on the wild rose stock. and the flaps of bark are closed over it. (5) The implantation is bound tightly with raffia: or special budding ties may be used. (6) Binding is removed. and the top of the stock is cut off in the following spring.

that every plant propagated will develop in time into a good plant. With roses, that is usually untrue. The poor ones should be burned without mercy, and only the strong ones kept. That is, unless anyone is content to spend the future suckling weaklings.

The form of propagation requiring least equipment is to take hard wood cuttings in late summer or autumn, insert them in the open ground or under a frame. They form callus over winter, begin rooting next spring, and are dug up and transplanted the following autumn.

Make the cuttings about 18 to 20 cm (7 to 8 in.) long, from ripe wood of the current season's growth. There is no need to remove any eyes, unless the cuttings are designed to provide stocks for budding on to. Dip them in rooting hormone, and plant them closely, two-thirds of the length buried, one-third exposed. The success rate varies enormously between varieties.

Most roses can be rooted from soft wood cuttings in spring and summer, given the proper conditions of humidity and heat. This implies that a greenhouse and mist unit are available. The best pieces to root are growing tips about 5 cm (2 in.) long; but lower portions of young wood, containing

The new shoot. or scion. should have its tip pinched out as soon as it has reached 6–8 cm (2½–3½ in.) in length. so that new shoots will form from the base.

two or three eyes, can also be rooted. This is an excellent way of propagating miniatures.

The commercial method of propagation is called budding. It consists of implanting one eye of the rose one wishes to multiply upon the root of a host plant. The top growth of the host plant is subsequently cut off, and within a year, the single eye has become a plant upon its foreign roots.

The host plant is known as the stock (or rootstock or understock). It is usually a seedling from a wild rose, although rooted cuttings of both wild and cultivated roses will serve.

The eye is known as the scion. It may be found in the upper angle where the leaf stalk joins the stem. Eyes selected for use are those which have not shot away, and are on young wood of recent growth. A fair guide (in the case of remontant roses) to the stage at which to select eyes, is that the shoot bears a bud or young bloom. Therefore the time is established as summer, and preferably early summer.

The method is as follows. Plant the stock in the autumn or spring beforehand. When ready to bud, remove soil to expose the main stem of the roots, immediately below the place where the stems of the aerial growth originate. Make two cuts through its bark, with a really sharp knife, to form the letter T, the crosscut about a third of the way round the circumference, the vertical cut to fit the eye, usually 2 to 3 cm ($\frac{3}{4}$ to $1\frac{1}{4}$ in.) long. The bark should then be slightly parted from the white wood inside it.

Now prepare the eye. Shorten the leaf stalk to a few millimeters, and cut a thin sliver of bark, with the eye in the center of it. The piece should be 2 or 3 cm long. Inside there will be a thin sliver of wood, which flips out when the point of the knife is placed between it and the bark. The eye is now ready, and can be slid (right way up!) into the T cut, so that the flaps of the down piece enclose it. Trim it off level with the crosscut, if it is too long. Bind the wound closely with raffia, or with a budding tie made for this purpose.

Stock and scion should be united in three weeks. The top of the stock should be cut off next spring, before growth starts. When the scion is 6 to 8 cm (2 to 3 in.) high, it is well to pinch out its tip, to make it shoot from the base, and to lessen the risk of its being blown out by the wind before its wood has hardened.

Hybridizers continue to create new rose varieties, which are budded onto wild rose stocks and roots for propagation. 'Escapade,' a rosy magenta violet Floribunda with a white center, dates from 1967.

ROSE PETAL WINE

4 liters (quarts) scented rose petals
4 liters water
$1\frac{1}{2}$ kg (3 lbs) white sugar
1 orange
1 lemon
yeast

Gather the petals on a dry sunny day, put them in a container, and pour over them the syrup made of the sugar and water. When cool enough, add the yeast and the juices from the fruit. Cover with a thin cloth, and leave nine days, stirring well once each day. Then strain into a clean jar, insert a fermentation lock, and keep comfortable until fermentation ceases. Strain into a clean jar and keep cold for two weeks, then continue as for Rose Hip Wine (from*). This wine has a beautiful rosy bouquet. It is equally good made with red or white and yellow petals. The white and yellow produce a pleasant white Bordeaux type of wine; the red, a rosé and usually more fragrant wine.

Cinderella

64

63   Baby Masquerade

Penelope   65

66 Cornelia

67 New Penny

69 Sweet Fairy

70 Starina

93

71 Compassion

73   Mme Grégoire Staechelin

74   Ena Harkness, Climbing

75 Altissimo

76 Bantry Bay

96

78   Golden Showers

Pink Perpetue

Baby Faurax 80

82 Handel

81 Pompon de Paris, Climbing

99

83 Yesterday

Félicité et Perpétue 84

85   Mozart

86   Ballerina

87 May Queen

New Dawn 88

90 Rosa Gallica Versicolor

62

BUFF BEAUTY

Hybrid Musk

This rose grows into a shrub chest-high or more, with double flowers the color of whitened honey. The petals are many and narrow, forming an open double flower, no pointed center to it, rather untidy, but in keeping with the old-fashioned look of the plant. The blooms are in clusters and look small until fully expanded, when the many petals against dull small leaves give a greater impression of size. 'Buff Beauty' flowers intermittently summer and autumn; it does not usually have a great outburst.
There is less fragrance than one would expect. It is a plant for a sleepy, summery corner of the garden.
It was introduced in England in 1939, but if there was a satisfactory account of its origin, it appears to have been lost. The general presumption is that it came from the Rev. J. Pemberton, of Hybrid Musk fame; but he had died more than ten years before 1939.

63

BABY MASQUERADE
syn BABY CARNAVAL

Miniature

A little bushy plant, with plenty of tiny leaves and small double flowers.
The buds are red; the flowers open light yellow, and then become flushed with pink on the outside petals; at times a cluster can therefore look parti-colored.
This is an easy Miniature to grow, for although dwarfish, it is vigorous, in the sense of growing freely within the limits of its nature.
The flowers are formed of about 28 small petals, showing a pretty form when young, but rather fluffy and indeterminate when fully expanded. No fragrance to speak of.
This rose was raised in Germany by Mathias Tantau from 'Peon' × 'Masquerade' and introduced in 1956.
It must be admitted that many Miniatures, although small in growth and leaf, fail to reproduce the daintiness of a sweet rose bloom on a small scale. The flowers are all too often shaggy when open.

64

CINDERELLA

Miniature

An almost perfect little Miniature, white with a touch of blush, and bearing some small carmine marks. The flowers are formed delightfully of about 50 petals, just like a thimble-sized Hybrid Tea while young, opening full. As should be the case in a Miniature, all the parts are scaled down in size, including the leaves. The growth is very short, almost thornless, especially on the upper parts of the plant. A spicy scent may be detected.
'Cinderella' was raised in Holland by John de Vink from 'Cécile Brunner' × 'Peon' and introduced in 1952.
Like many Miniatures, 'Cinderella' is an exquisite rose to grow in a pot. The plants should be grown outside the house, either in the open or in a frame or in a glasshouse, and only brought indoors when they are showing blooms. They are not house plants, and must go outside again into the daylight.

65

PENELOPE

Hybrid Musk

This clean-cut, simple beauty is a shrub about hip high, with small semi-double flowers of shell pink, carried in incredible profusion in summer. Each one is unsophisticated, just two rows of petals around yellow stamens, issuing a gentle fragrance, the whole backed by honest green leaves. 'Penelope' is as refreshing as a shower on a hot day.

After the summer flush, it is necessary to take the dead heads off, in order to encourage some flowers for autumn; otherwise the bushes will be a vast mass of hips, with little bloom to come. Of course, one can opt for the hips instead, but they color brown rather than red.

It was raised in England by the Rev. Joseph Pemberton and introduced in 1924. The seed parent is believed to have been 'Ophelia.'

Although looked upon as a shrub rose today, this and other Hybrid Musks were formerly used for bedding.

66

CORNELIA

Hybrid Musk

A fine, handsome shrub, head-high and nearly twice as wide, filling up space generously (or greedily, if the garden is small). Its dark leaves make it a fine mask in the garden and provide a good backing for the clusters of pink flowers which are small, semi-double, and fragrant.

The color is usually described as strawberry pink, and there is a touch of yellow at the petal's base. 'Cornelia' is remontant, the plant not fully covered in flower, but normally bearing some color. Good in autumn.

This rose was raised in England by the Rev. Joseph Pemberton and introduced in 1925.

Many old plants of it are thriving around the world. It may usually be recognized by the dark look its leaves impart to the shrub. Such a plant, if bearing small pink flowers and growing large, is most likely 'Cornelia.' The name Hybrid Musk is not accurate, for they are not Musk.

67

NEW PENNY

Miniature

This little plant fairly glitters; for its small dark leaves are polished glossy to reflect the sun, and the little red buds stand up smartly. A nice little tussock of a plant: vigorous and as bright as its name implies.

The red buds do not produce red flowers, but in fact light pink ones, which open their 20 petals into a little circle, stamens showing in the middle beautifully. There is some scent, but in general one does not notice the scent of Miniatures, short of lifting them up, or going down to them on hands and knees.

'New Penny' was raised by Ralph S. Moore in California from two unnamed seedlings; it was introduced in 1962. The normal description is orange-red to coral-pink, but it is not so highly colored.

It has been widely used in breeding subsequent Miniatures. Its raiser, Ralph Moore, has dedicated himself to this type of rose.

68

ROSINA syn
JOSEPHINE WHEATCROFT

Miniature

The name was changed, because this has been for years the best yellow Miniature, whereas its Spanish name makes it sound more like a pink rose in English. Although there are not many petals (about 16), the buds are perfectly formed, little golden yellow jewels, tiny copies of Hybrid Teas.

They naturally open semi-double, but, while in their bud form, they are perfect for a great many decorative uses.

The plants are short and bushy, not quite as compact as the other Miniatures we have described; the small foliage of deep grassy green goes well with the flowers. There is little scent.

Raised in Spain from 'Eduardo Toda' × 'Rouletii' by Pedro Dot, this Miniature was introduced in Britain, France, and the United States in 1951 by Wheatcroft, Meilland, and the Conard-Pyle Company respectively. It is the best yellow to date.

69

SWEET FAIRY

Miniature

This reliable pink Miniature has been a favorite since the modern interest in Miniatures awoke. It is a small plant indeed, whose tiny flowers contain an amazing number of petals, about 60. The color is light pink, and the scent is pleasant, not strong. It has lovely miniature rose leaves.

With so many petals, 'Sweet Fairy' is too full to imitate the Hybrid Tea shape of flower. Imagine it as a pin cushion, stuck with little old-fashioned roses, narrow petaled and sweetly pink.

It was raised in Holland by John de Vink from 'Peon' × Seedling and introduced in 1946.

John de Vink was a pioneer in Miniatures. He began to work on 'Rouletii,' which was the surviving Miniature from the nineteenth century, and which, after being lost, was found in Switzerland about 1918. He bred 'Rouletii' with Polyanthas, to obtain narrow petals.

70

STARINA

Miniature

This may claim to be one of the most colorful Miniatures, genuinely a short bedding rose, with abundant orange scarlet flowers covering the little plants. The flowers are double, small, well formed with a low pointed center, the outer petals well expanded. The color of the young flowers is quite dazzling, but they fade to some extent before falling, and can well be trimmed off. It is better to dispense with a few days of faded flower, and at the same time accelerate the arrival of the next crop. There is not much scent.

This is a French variety, raised by Mme Louisette Meilland from Seedling × 'Perla de Montserrat' and introduced in 1965.

Many breeders are interested in Miniatures, because they are easily marketable as pot plants. Their aim is to produce rounded plants to grow in pots. But the real work for the breeders is to make the flowers like tiny Hybrid Teas.

71

COMPASSION

Climbing Hybrid Tea

Here is a beautifully fragrant climbing rose, pink, with lively salmon-orange shading, to a degree that varies. The flowers, which have about 39 petals, are well formed like Hybrid Teas but a little smaller. They appear freely in summer and autumn.

The growth is vigorous, usually producing many basal shoots; it is suitable for a house wall, fence, or post. The leaves are glossy dark green, abundant, and handsome.

It was raised in England by the author from 'White Cockade' × 'Prima Ballerina' and introduced in 1973.

Climbers cover all sorts of objects, and in general, the larger the plant, the shorter its flowering period. The demand now is for remontant climbers; that is to say, they flower twice or oftener in the season. It follows that they do not grow quite so far, because their shoots terminate in a bud, instead of going onward.

72

ROYAL GOLD

Climbing Hybrid Tea

A climber with large yellow flowers is certainly desirable, and many of them have been offered, accepted for a while, and found wanting. This one is certainly wanting in vigor and hardiness, but in those places where it is not exposed to bitter weather, and can enjoy the favors of fertility, it should be successful.

The flowers are deep yellow, with stately conical centers; both color and form are first class. There are about 32 petals. Fragrance is fruity, not very strong. The plants, of moderate vigor, are not noted for freedom of flower. People are so pleased with one when they get it, that 'Royal Gold' is forgiven its sins.

It was raised by Dr. Dennison Morey in California from 'Climbing Goldilocks' × 'Lydia' and introduced by Jackson and Perkins in 1957.

The two parents had rather flat flowers, but have produced a long flower.

73

Mme GRÉGOIRE STAECHELIN
syn SPANISH BEAUTY

Climbing Hybrid Tea

A dramatic sight in early summer, when its wide flowers are open to show the peculiar ruffled edge of the petals, and the plant is a sea of rich pink, the big flowers jostling one another for a twig hold, and shedding scent like a perfume shop being looted.
Put such a sight on a wall or fence, and for a couple of weeks your garden will outshine the beauty of the Taj Mahal itself. Once the petals have fallen thick on the ground below, there will be no more flowers at all until next summer—only fat rose hips, and the memory of the wide ruffled skirts of this Spanish beauty.
It was raised in Spain by Pedro Dot from 'Frau Karl Druschki' × 'Château de Clos Vougeot' and introduced in 1927.
The two parents were very popular. 'Frau Karl Druschki' is still grown as a white rose. 'Château de Clos Vougeot' was darkest red, but a weakly grower. They produced a winner.

74

ENA HARKNESS,
CLIMBING

Climbing Hybrid Tea

One of the world's most famous red roses, 'Ena Harkness' can still be grown as a bush, but is perhaps even better as a climber. The tendency for the flowers to nod on the stems is then an advantage, for they bow to meet the gaze.
The beautiful crimson color has never been surpassed, and it is allied to a particularly lovely flower form, the petals being slightly parted at the center, without losing any of their beauty and dignity. There are about 30 petals. The climbing form is an excellent plant for walls and fences; the summer flowering is early and copious; the autumn flowering is spasmodic.
The bush was raised in England by Albert Norman from 'Crimson Glory' × 'Southport' and introduced in 1946. The climber appeared in two English nurseries and was introduced in 1954. Bushes sometimes climb thanks to their ancestry.

75

ALTISSIMO

Climbing Floribunda

Large red flowers, of only five or seven petals, present a special kind of beauty, as lovely in its way as that given by many-petaled flowers. The stamens act as a yellow focal point to the red; this is especially effective when there are a number of blooms showing at the same time.

Climbers such as 'Altissimo' need to be trained horizontally to achieve their best effect (as suggested in the sketch shown here). This is an excellent rose for a post, a wall, or a fence. It is rarely a mass of bloom, but rather intermittent through summer and autumn. There is not much scent.
'Altissimo' was raised in France by Georges Delbard from seed of a climber called 'Ténor' and introduced in 1966.

76

BANTRY BAY

Climbing Floribunda

With an air of humility, because there is nothing brash about its rose pink flowers, 'Bantry Bay' can decorate a wall or pillar so as to set an example to most other climbers. The shoots are easy to train, and the growth is normally appropriate to the restricted wall space on most modern homes.
The plant is adept at covering itself in bloom evenly and generously, without crowding the flowers in one place, or leaving large blank patches in others. It is remontant.
The semi-double flowers open pleasantly wide, to color more space than might have been expected from the buds. There is a color change from bud to open bloom; but the fresh rose pink of the mature blooms is even more pleasing than the deeper color of the young ones. One could wish for more scent. Raised by Sam McGredy from 'New Dawn' × 'Korona,' it was introduced in 1967.

108

77

78

79

80

DANSE DU FEU
syn SPECTACULAR

Climbing Floribunda

One of the most free-flowering climbers, with the unusual gift of being able to cover itself with flowers, even as a small plant in a confined space; or equally if it has grown larger. This freedom is shown both in summer and autumn. The flowers are bright scarlet and not very large, with about 32 petals. The form is somewhat rounded, eventually opening flat, and the flowers are borne in clusters. There is not much scent, and the color is apt to turn unpleasantly purple when the flowers are old.
Raised in France by the distinguished French amateur, Charles Mallerin. He bred it from seed of 'Paul's Scarlet Climber'; it was introduced in France in 1953, and in the United States in 1956.
It is a fine plant for a fence or wall, being resistant to disease and free flowering. It will not, as a rule, climb a great distance. Its distribution must now be worldwide.

GOLDEN SHOWERS

Climbing Floribunda

Free-flowering and yellow, two good points; but only just a climber. It is really a bush, which responds to being planted on a support by gradually covering it. The flowers are clear yellow, forming attractive pointed buds. They open very quickly, having only about 20 petals, into semi-double flowers, which can be wide, and are especially attractive when they reveal the young stamens. 'Golden Showers,' which blooms freely in summer and autumn, has a fresh but not powerful scent; it blooms on long stems, and is adorned with glossy dark green leaves.
It was raised in the United States by Dr. Walter E. Lammerts from 'Charlotte Armstrong' × 'Capt. Thomas' and introduced by Germain's Nursery of Los Angeles in 1956. 'Charlotte Armstrong' is seed parent to many fine roses, including 'Queen Elizabeth,' 'Sutter's Gold,' 'Mojave,' and 'First Love.' All these are American.

PINK PERPETUE

Climbing Floribunda

A vigorous climber within a small space, for it is rarely seen to grow very tall; its stems are quite stiff, and they carry a tremendous number of double pink blooms, both in summer and autumn. The flowers are well formed of 32 petals, not very large, colored deep rose pink with a touch of carmine.
This rose may be grown on a wall or fence, or even as a shrub; it has not much scent.
It was raised in England by Walter Gregory from 'Danse du Feu' × 'New Dawn' and introduced in 1965.
At the same time Mr. Gregory had a sister seedling called 'Etude,' from the same parents. This had a prettier color than 'Pink Perpetue,' and a larger flower. But it had nothing like the amount of bloom, and accordingly was relegated to comparative obscurity. The worst fault of 'Pink Perpetue' is that the color is hard, but not everyone will think so.

BABY FAURAX

Polyantha

If the photographer and printer succeed in copying nature, the picture of this rose ought to be colored amethyst; it is as blue as any rose, but all too often it mysteriously emerges through the printing works a dirty pink.
The flowers are very small, double, with about 45 short petals; these lever themselves halfway open, showing plenty of dusty pollen, and stay there until they drop. They do not lose much color, there's a lightening of it, but it is possible to mistake an almost shattering 'Baby Faurax' for a young one. The plants are stumpy, very poor things, rising with reluctance only a little way from the earth. Try growing it as a pot plant for its unique color; and it has pleasant fragrance too.
'Baby Faurax' was raised in France by Leonard Lille and introduced in 1924. No parents were listed. It is possible it could be a dwarf sport from a rambler, e.g. 'Veilchenblau.'

81

POMPON DE PARIS, CLIMBING

Climbing Miniature

This splendid plant would be grown everywhere, if it did not utterly refuse to be remontant. Unfortunately it confines itself to flower only in early summer. Well, it is so beautiful then that it is worth its place, especially upon a low garden wall, or a terrace, or even a house wall. Although a Miniature, it will grow like mad, farther than many other climbers. The miniature flowers are pink, rosy, and warm; they open into little double pompons with many petals and crowd densely upon the branches. That glorious sight is backed by myriads of tiny leaves, gleaming bright and dark as they efficiently furnish a lovely plant.

The origin is not known. Presumably it sported in a French glasshouse in the nineteenth century. Miniatures were grown by the thousand for the flower markets in Paris and London. Then the fashion changed and they were set aside, until 1918.

82

HANDEL

Climbing Floribunda

The art of flushing and rimming a flower is shown most beautifully here, for the creamy flowers of 'Handel' are marked rose red, particularly at the edges of the petals. As the flowers are of good medium size, and nicely shaped out of their 22 petals, the colors they wear are such as to command notice.

This vigorous modern climber is one of the best for walls, fences, large posts, or to cover small structures. It is remontant; that is, it flowers twice or more in the season. Although less fragrant than it looks, it has a pleasant scent; it is an effective cut flower.

It was raised in Northern Ireland by Sam McGredy from 'Columbine' × 'Heidelberg' and introduced in 1965.

'Heidelberg' is a bright crimson shrub rose, often known as a Hybrid Musk, although not truly one. It is susceptible to blackspot, a trait shared by 'Handel' to a lesser extent.

83

YESTERDAY
syn TAPIS d'ORIENT

Polyantha

Most people have never seen a rose like this: the airy clusters contain dozens of little flowers, each one consisting of about 13 narrow petals, which open quite flat around the dusty stamens. The flowers are lively pink, changing beautifully to lavender pink; a coin would cover one of them.

The leaves are small, and the bushes graceful, with an occasional shoot rising high. The fragrance is sweet, as may best be tested by cutting a spray and taking it into one's room. It can make a delightful, if irregular, hedge and it flowers remontantly and generously.

It was raised in England from Seedling × 'Ballerina' by the author and introduced in 1974.

The parent seedling was from 'Phyllis Bide,' a climber, which in turn came from 'Perle d'Or,' which is from China and Polyantha roses. Thus 'Yesterday' has Polyantha on both parental sides.

84

FÉLICITÉ ET PERPÉTUE

Sempervirens Hybrid

A beautiful white climber, bred from the wild Evergreen Rose. It has small double flowers which are rather flat, with the center closely surrounded by rows of petals, not much space between them. The color is white, with some rose red flecks. It looks pure and beautiful.

The growth is very strong; there is many a cottage decked with this old white rose, with its slightly blue-green foliage persisting long into the winter. It is not remontant and has only a little scent.

It was raised in France by A. A. Jacques and introduced in 1827.

A beautiful bush rose, which is a dwarf form of this climber, is 'Little White Pet'; it is remontant, and has the same pretty little double flowers. It was introduced by Henderson of New York in 1879; it grows like a bushy, short Floribunda; an unusual white rose, well worth growing, the sort of plant one becomes fond of.

85

MOZART

Polyantha

This twin sister of 'Ballerina' has long been popular in Continental Europe, and it was not until a year or two ago that the two varieties were carefully compared. For many years they had been taken to be the same.

The differences are soon seen. 'Mozart' is deeper pink than 'Ballerina' around its pale middle, and its leaves are larger and not so shiny. Otherwise, the description for 'Ballerina' fits it.

This other "phlox-like" rose was raised in Germany by Peter Lambert from 'Robin Hood' × 'Rote Pharisäer.' Curiously, it was also introduced in 1937.

The 'Ballerina' and 'Mozart' types are those of modern Polyanthas. This class is distinguished by its small flowers, and general affinity to *R. multiflora.* Formerly it consisted of many small plants, known as Polyantha Pompons, and for the greater part, sports of one another.

86

BALLERINA

Polyantha

As easy to grow as any rose, 'Ballerina' has great heads of tiny flowers of five petals, each one about the size of a phlox. Many people do not recognize it as a rose. It grows as a shrub about hip high, very compact, with many small glossy leaves to back its hundreds of flowers. A fine hedge can be made of it, and it flowers in summer and autumn.

The flowers, pale as apple blossom, grow still lighter at the center. There is no scent; and in their eagerness to remain at their posts, and give full value, the blooms may have to be trimmed off when they are seen to be sere and old.

It was raised in England by J. A. Bentall and introduced in 1937, the parents not being known.

A red variety has recently been introduced under the name 'Marjorie Fair.' It is sold in Holland as 'Red Ballerina,' although there is an English rose so called, but not the same at all, being half a Floribunda.

87

MAY QUEEN

Wichuraiana Hybrid

A pretty pink climbing rose, with charming flowers of old-fashioned appearance. They are quartered; that is to say, the heart of the flower, instead of looking like a cone, is actually wrapped into four segments. This was the case with many old roses, which thereby got their special charm.

The flowers, less than medium size, appear freely in early summer; there is little or no autumn bloom and not much fragrance either. Growth is restrained, very suitable for a fence or post.

This was one of the early climbers raised in the United States, in this case by W. A. Manda of New Jersey, from *R. wichuraiana* × 'Champion of the World.' It was introduced in 1898. American breeders did much to develop climbing roses; men such as Michael Horvath of Mentor, Ohio; M. H. Walsh of Wood's Hole, Mass.; the little known Mr. Miller, with 'Dorothy Perkins.'

88

NEW DAWN

Wichuraiana Hybrid

A famous rose of palest pearl pink, its young blooms beautifully pointed, and breathing out fragrance as though to purify the world. It is usually grown as a climber, especially on posts or fences; but for anyone who can spare the room, it is better still as a shrub and will cover itself in blossom like a bride in her wedding dress.

The flowers are less than medium size, and open semi-double. They are useful for cutting and mix well with many common garden flowers in a vase.

'New Dawn' has a reputation of being remontant, but its autumn flower is usually very much less than summer.

It was discovered as a less vigorous and more remontant mutation of 'Dr. W. van Fleet' in the Somerset Rose Nurseries in New Jersey and was introduced in 1930.

It was the holder of U.S. Plant Patent No. 1; good for seventeen years.

89

ALBÉRIC BARBIER

Wichuraiana Hybrid

This cream climber, with glossy leaves and long, trailing branches, is to be seen on house walls and fences, growing over porches and all sorts of objects. The chances are that everybody who has seen roses growing in gardens has seen 'Albéric Barbier.' It is a long-lived plant, with tenacity to survive in adverse places. The buds are small and yellow, opening into medium-size flowers, which are white, with some yellow deep in the center of them. The middle petals are narrow, the form confused, the fragrance moderate. It flowers well in summer and has also a few flowers in the autumn. The growth is long and vigorous; the plant will cover a large area.

It was raised in France by Barbier and Cie from the wild *R. wichuraiana* × 'Shirley Hibberd' and was introduced in 1900. Americans know *R. wichuraiana* as the Memorial rose; it has shiny leaves.

90

R. GALLICA VERSICOLOR
syn ROSA MUNDI

Gallicanae

This striped rose has been famous for at least 300 years; its alternations of red and blush are clearly shown, because the flowers open out flat to exhibit the full length of their striped petals; and the yellow stamens highlight the pretty flowers beautifully. There are about 12 petals, and the flowers are of medium size, with a fresh but not powerful scent. The bushes flower only once in the season, in summer, and are well covered with matt green leaves, which are likely to get mildew, especially when the flowers are over. The stems are closely covered with bristles.

Various theories exist about the origin of this rose. It is obviously a mutation of the red *R. gallica officinalis;* one account says it first occurred in England about 1650, but some students claim to identify it with roses described in old books before that date. Nobody can be perfectly sure of the answer now.

91

LEVERKUSEN

Kordesii Hybrid

A reliable yellow climber, which one can plant in expectation of pleasant sulfur-yellow flowers duly arriving every summer and autumn without much trouble. It provides good background color, but has little claim to ethereal beauty and joy. The flowers are semi-double, well pointed in the buds and young blooms; but when they fully open, their appearance must be confessed shaggy.

The fragrance is slight; the leaves are small, individually handsome but not over-plentiful.

It is one of a famous group of roses raised in Germany by Wilhelm Kordes; this came from *R. kordesii* × 'Golden Glow' and was introduced in 1954.

The origin of *R. kordesii* was a trailing rose discovered in America and called 'Max Graf.' Although not very fertile, it produced the seed which developed into *R. kordesii*. This proved a new and valuable tool for breeders.

92

THE FAIRY

Wichuraiana Hybrid

Quite different from the other Wichuraianas we have described, this is a bush whereas they are primarily climbers. 'The Fairy' has so much fresh beauty to offer: its flowers are plentiful, small, and light pink, perfectly backed by the dark polish of myriad tiny leaves. The bushes are usually low and spreading at first, growing bigger over some years. It is well into summer before 'The Fairy' flowers, usually when most roses are going past their first flush. The little flowers have about 25 petals and open to a coin-sized circle, with a few stamens looking out among the central pieces of pink. Slight fragrance only; but a pleasing rose to cut.

A mutation from 'Lady Godiva,' a rambling rose, 'The Fairy' was discovered in England and introduced by J. A. Bentall in 1932; and in America by the Conard-Pyle Company in 1941. It makes a fine standard.

THE ROSE BREEDERS

A triumph of the breeder's art: the remarkable 'Peace,' a gold and yellow Hybrid Tea—also known as 'Mme A. Meilland,' 'Gloria Dei,' 'Gioia' in various countries. Introduced in 1942, 'Peace' was an immediate success and, by the mid-1950s, was being grown all over the world, with an estimated 30 million plants in existence. This famous modern rose has been named the favorite in several worldwide polls.

No aspect of rose growing is more fascinating than breeding new varieties; and although at first sight it appears a specialized and complex subject, it is in reality simplicity itself, and may readily be understood with a little consideration of how plants grow.

The process of growth is like bricklaying, the bricks being living plant cells whose layers are constantly added to until the structure is complete. The main difference from bricks is that the cells are self-generative, and increase by dividing themselves into two. This goes on at a great rate in times of full growth, and is complicated by the different types of growth required—for example, stem, bark, thorn, leaf, petal, seed.

The orders to make the kind of leaf or petal characteristic of the variety are carried in the genetic particles; these are borne upon thread-like organisms called chromosomes, of which an identical set (usually 14 or 28) exists in every cell of a rose plant, except for the sexual cells.

So that the new cell may be a genetic replica of the old, each chromosome splits into twins before the moment of cell division, and one of each twin departs to opposite ends of the cell; there each group is divided by a new cell wall, to form two cells, each of the same chromosome content as the former.

These facts account for the first means of rose breeding: when so many thousands of millions of divisions occur, there will be an occasional accident; and if the accident concerns a chromosome or genetic particle, it will normally become visible in the outward appearance of the plant, because the genetic particles give the orders for growth, down to the smallest detail.

Such accidents took place long before human beings inhabited the planet; and the sort of variations first noticed by mankind were probably flowers which had ten or fifteen petals where they should have had five, or flowers which were red or white instead of being pink, or plants which were dwarf or climbing although their proper nature was bushy.

The late Francis Meilland of France, creator of 'Peace,' was one of the best-known rose breeders. Thanks partly to his efforts, rose breeding became recognized as a specialized profession entitled to 'copyright' protection. The creation of a rose such as the famous 'Peace' is a long, painstaking process of trial-and-error that may require many thousands of cross-breedings.

One line of inquiry in breeding is to induce such accidents by drugs, or radiation, or other physical pressures. But the mainstream of breeding is otherwise, through the seed.

When the plant arrives at the point of growth which concerns reproduction, it modifies its method of cell division. A sexual union is in prospect, to constitute the plant's child, which is the seed. In a sexual union, male and female cells must fuse; but if a plant of 14 chromosomes fuses two such cells, then the offspring will have 28 chromosomes, which is absurd, for in a few generations it would have thousands. So the male cells (namely the pollen grains) and the female (or egg cells) are both reduced to 7 chromosomes. Thus they may fuse to reconstitute the correct 14.

In the case of a wild rose, both male and female genetic particles are exactly the same, and so the seedling grows exactly as the parent plant did. But from very early times it happened that the pollen of one wild rose fertilized a different wild rose, having been carried by insects or through the air. Then the seed was composed of a different mixture of genetic particles, and its character was necessarily different from that of its parents.

The interplay of genetic particles from different parents is complex, and not completely understood. It is at least clear that there are so many genetic particles as to produce a huge number of permutations; and as far as our human capability of exploring them is concerned, we may at present say that the number of possible variations is as good as infinite.

Therefore rose breeders deliberately convey the pollen from one rose to another, and grow the seed which is the result. Each seedling is different, if only slightly; and therefore there is at the beginning only one plant of a new variety. That one plant is propagated vegetatively, usually by budding or grafting, until it is eventually, like 'Peace,' multiplied by millions.

It was only fairly late in the nineteenth century that pollen was deliberately transferred as a general practice. Up to that time, even though the method was known, breeders used to leave pollination to the insects and the wind. The first convincing demonstration of a better way was in 1879 by Henry Bennett, an English cattle breeder, who turned his hand to breeding roses and called his new roses "Pedigree": a good farming touch.

This demonstration by an Englishman was quickly absorbed in France, then the center of rose breeding. But it was also taken to heart within a few years by Dickson in Northern Ireland; McGredy, also of Northern Ireland, followed about 1905; and Poulsen in Denmark, about the same time.

Wilhelm Kordes of Germany: another important name in the history of rose cultivation.

'Ena Harkness,' crimson Hybrid Tea, was raised by A. Norman, 1946.

'Crimson Glory,' a Hybrid Tea introduced by W. Kordes in 1935.

British amateur Albert Norman has made lasting contributions to the rose world.

'Grandpa Dickson syn Irish Gold,' Hybrid Tea: from P. Dickson, 1966.

Sam McGredy, a Northern Irishman transplanted to New Zealand, has many important roses to his credit.

'Chinatown,' Floribunda, gold tinged with red, introduced by N. Poulsen in 1962.

Much can be learned about rose breeding by considering its leading living practitioners. One fact to emerge at once is that they are nearly all nurserymen, often following their fathers and grandfathers. In their establishments, roses were bred in order to furnish the business with new varieties; there was no living to be made by breeding alone; nevertheless it became a way of life.

The Dickson family produced a long series of successful roses, with a marked leaning toward Hybrid Teas of very perfect form. There is an element in breeding of "Seek and ye shall find." Patrick Dickson's two most successful varieties at present are Hybrid Teas in the family tradition, the yellow 'Grandpa Dickson syn Irish Gold' and the light crimson 'Red Devil.'

He has also sought red Hybrid Teas of better foliage and vigor than ever before, and may perhaps have done all the groundwork for the great red rose of the future, if, as one hopes, it may be bred from his line. 'Red Planet' and 'Precious Platinum syn Red Star' show the direction he has taken.

Sam McGredy was denied the chance of learning from his father, as Dickson did, because he was a child when his father died. Emerging from college, he joined the family firm, whereupon he was given the keys of the greenhouses and told to get on with it. Fortunately he had the energy and intelligence to equip himself with the necessary knowledge, and within a few years was raising roses such as 'Mischief' and 'Piccadilly,' which went all over the world. More than most nurserymen, he has been a specialist breeder, leaving the ordinary nursery work to others; he emigrated to New Zealand in 1972, confident that the climate would expedite his work. A classic example in breeding is his vision from the white eye of 'Frühlingsmorgen,' which eventually led him, through some most unpromising generations, into the red and white patterns of 'Picasso,' 'Matangi,' and 'Priscilla Burton.'

The Poulsen family in Denmark sought hardy roses for northern Europe; in using Polyanthas (for hardiness) with Hybrid Teas (for beauty) they gave the world the gift of Floribundas. It was again a case of the younger generation learning from the older, the most recent transference being from Niels Dines Poulsen to his daughter, Pernille Olesen. Among the famous recent roses from Niels Poulsen are 'Chinatown' and 'Troika syn Royal Dane.'

Two famous German breeders grew in fame in the twentieth century: Tantau of Uetersen and Kordes of Sparrieshoop. Mathias Tantau typically says that he was in the fortunate

Patrick Dickson of Northern Ireland has specialized in Hybrid Teas.

'Picasso,' a recent creation of Sam McGredy.

Niels Dines Poulsen, of the famous Danish family of rose breeders.

Mathias Tantau, one of the greatest German breeders of our century.

'Peer Gynt,' a yellow and pink Hybrid Tea, by Reimer Kordes, 1968.

Gijsbert de Ruiter, a prominent Dutch breeder.

'Prima Ballerina,' a pink Hybrid Tea, was introduced by Tantau in 1957.

Reimer Kordes has followed in the distinguished footsteps of his father, Wilhelm.

The Floribunda 'Orange Sensation,' by de Ruiter, 1960.

position of finding in his father a good teacher. He had a marvelous series of triumphs in the 1960s, with 'Super Star syn Tropicana,' 'Duftwolke syn Fragrant Cloud,' 'Mainzer Fastnacht syn Blue Moon,' and 'Prima Ballerina.' The origin of 'Super Star' is not quite clear, which is a pity, because in color and foliage it would appear to have an interesting background. The species *R. multibracteata* has been mentioned as an ancestor; and it can be noted that as 'Super Star' is a late flowering Hybrid Tea, so *R. multibracteata* is a late flowering species.

No breeder of the twentieth century gave more to the world of roses than Wilhelm Kordes. His 'Crimson Glory' was not only his most successful rose, but a useful parent for contemporary Hybrid Teas and Floribundas. But a breeder's greatest success is not necessarily his most popular rose. Kordes brought the vivid pelargonium scarlet into modern roses, through a variety called 'Baby Château.' He used the Sweet Briar 'Magnifica' for hardiness, matched it with yellows, and brought revivifying strength into yellow Hybrid Teas and Floribundas. He persevered with the almost sterile 'Max Graf,' until it gave him the highly fertile *R. kordesii*, and led valuable new elements of health and hardiness into modern roses. These are but a few instances of his genius. With such a father to teach him, Reimer Kordes has brilliantly upheld the family tradition, as witness his great roses, 'Schneewittchen syn Iceberg,' 'Lilli Marlene,' 'Friesia syn Korresia,' 'Peer Gynt,' and many more. Like his father, his view is wide, and he seeks roses for all the uses to which they can possibly be put, a program of so many wishes that he himself says they cannot be filled in a human lifetime.

In 1914 a Dutchman named Gerrit de Ruiter found a red sport of the pink Polyantha 'Orléans Rose'; and it was eventually introduced as 'Miss Edith Cavell.' The Polyanthas were generous in sporting, and De Ruiter adept at detecting them, for he introduced one after another, culminating in the vermilion 'Gloria Mundi.' He therefore began to breed in earnest by pollination, a practice followed by two of his sons. So firmly were their fortunes founded on their original type of discovery, that the firm incorporated "Rosa Polyantha" in its address.

Gijsbert de Ruiter, continuing his father's work, has become a breeder of international reputation, with a special eye on roses for the Scandinavian market, including those which can be grown as pot plants. Some of his famous varieties are the Floribunda 'Orange Sensation' and the Hybrid Tea 'Diorama.' Out of his researches for pot roses came the Polyantha 'Ocaru syn Angela Rippon.'

Louisette Meilland, of the French rose-breeding dynasty, is one of the few women breeders to achieve prominence.

'Sonia Meilland syn Sweet Promise,' created by A. Meilland, introduced 1973.

Herbert Swim, of the Armstrong Nurseries in California, was active in the postwar years.

Among rose breeders, few names are better known than that of Meilland, from the south of France. While quite a young man, Francis Meilland had the astonishing success of 'Mme A. Meilland syn Peace,' of which the seed was formed in 1935. Although he had no means of knowing it without trial, that rose was to be one of the most successful parents of future Hybrid Teas, and Meilland was naturally the first to discover that fact. He had, therefore, a string of winners for twenty years to come, in fact for the rest of his short life. Added to these, he raised the most successful cut flower rose of his time in 'Baccara.'

Francis Meilland took the lead in pressing for a just reward to rose breeders, on the grounds that it was unheard of for an author to sell one book and have the world reproduce it free of charge. It is largely due to his work that plant breeders' rights were realized to be fair in principle, and slowly became accepted. Francis probably learned much from his father, but most of his training was from an amateur, a retired railwayman called Charles Mallerin.

Louisette Meilland, the widow of Francis, is also a breeder in her own right; thus their son Alain was able to complete from his mother what knowledge might have been interrupted by his father's early death. He is famous for his painstaking research into cut-flower roses, for not only does he breed them, but presents to the glasshouse growers much information as to culture and yield. His 'Sonia Meilland syn Sweet Promise' is to be seen in countless flower shops, for millions of its blooms pass annually through the markets. Among his garden roses are 'Papa Meilland' and the Miniatures 'Minuetto syn Darling Flame' and 'Starina.'

Many good roses came from America in the twentieth century, including 'Queen Elizabeth' from Dr. W. E. Lammerts, 'Sutter's Gold' and 'First Love' from Herbert Swim, and 'Pink Favorite' from Dr. Gordon von Abrams. The greatest scene of activity in that country at present is the Jackson and Perkins Co., whose rose breeder Eugene Boerner played a major part in establishing the popularity of Floribundas through such varieties as 'Goldilocks,' 'Fashion,' 'Masquerade,' and 'Spartan.' Their breeding program was probably the most ambitious ever attempted, with, according to breeders' gossip, a quarter of a million crosses being made in one year. The present rose breeder at J & P is William Warriner, who has a leaning toward cut-flower varieties, but has also produced some high-class garden roses, including 'Evening Star,' a beautiful white Hybrid Tea.

No statistics exist to show exactly how many crosses each

'Baccara,' a cut flower rose, is another outstanding creation by Francis Meilland, breeder of 'Peace.'

Alain Meilland, successor to an important family tradition.

'Sutter's Gold,' a yellow and red Hybrid Tea, by Herbert Swim, 1950.

breeder makes, but subject to that proviso, it would appear that the leading eight are those we have mentioned—namely, Jackson and Perkins, Kordes, Meilland, McGredy, Dickson, Tantau, Poulsen, and De Ruiter. To them may be added a ninth, one of the most recent to have entered the field, namely James Cocker and Sons of Aberdeen, Scotland. Theirs is a family nursery business, and like every one of the others, with the sole exception of Jackson and Perkins, was handed down from father to son for a number of generations.

Alexander Cocker began breeding roses in 1963, and in the remaining fourteen years of his life scored some tremendous successes, including the Hybrid Teas 'Alec's Red' and 'Silver Jubilee.' The latter is of particular importance, because the breeder used 'Parkdirektor Riggers' in order to breed the strain of *R. kordesii* into Hybrid Teas. It is only by the influx of fresh blood that a class such as the Hybrid Teas can be kept in health and strength. Upon the death of Mr. Cocker in 1977, his son Alexander, only seventeen, undertook to continue the firm's breeding. Like many nursery sons, he had been absorbing the craft of rose growing from the time he left his pram, and was already skilled in many operations, especially propagation; he also knew much of the breeding from his father.

A great number of rose breeders practice professionally on quite a small scale, but not necessarily with less success than the giants. Smallness indeed has advantages, because in a work which depends largely on observation by an individual with specialized knowledge, a small number of seedlings can be more thoroughly observed than a large one.

It is not generally realized how quick the process is, even though the average time from pollination to sale may be seven years. If we cross two roses in the summer of 1980, the seed is sown the following winter (usually in benches under glass) and will flower on its single shoot in the summer of 1981. At this stage, observation is vital, to recognize not only the winners (which is easy enough) but also those which may be a partway stage to the objective. That is difficult. No sign of the objective may be evident in the very seedling that could lead to it.

During that same summer of 1981, several eyes of the seedlings chosen for propagation are budded on to rootstocks growing out of doors; and these will flower as well-grown maiden plants in summer 1982. A breeder with long experience of growing roses for sale should therefore recognize the potentiality of his seedlings as garden plants two years from pollination time. He puts them to further trial, but also

Alexander Cocker of Scotland created a whole series of marvelous roses between 1963 and 1977.

Le Grice introduced 'Allgold,' a Floribunda, in 1956.

'Silver Jubilee,' a pink Hybrid Tea created by Alexander Cocker, was introduced, to tremendous acclaim, in 1978.

E. B. Le Grice, an English breeder, created roses in unusual hues.

'New Penny' is a red Miniature created by R. Moore in 1962.

Louis Lens of Belgium has been breeding roses since 1945.

'Altissimo,' a climbing Floribunda: Georges Delbard, 1966.

increases his stock of them, so that he is ready to sell them without further delay when he is satisfied by their performance; frequently, instead of selling them he burns them. Rose breeding is a production line which has no guarantee of ending with a saleable product. An able breeder usually achieves at least some part of his vision; but the random dispersal of the genetic particles leaves the final decision to Fortune.

A distinguished and thoughtful hybridist on modest scale was Edward Le Grice of Norfolk, England. His masterpiece was 'Allgold,' a yellow Floribunda which he sought for out of 'Goldilocks'; his aim was to raise a bright and unfading yellow rose. He patiently tried many yellow roses until he found parents to give the color he wanted in 'Ellinor Le Grice.' When pollen of that was transferred to 'Goldilocks,' the seed proved the fruit he wanted. 'Allgold' had an additional virtue of being resistant to blackspot.

Ralph Moore, of Visalia, California, has devoted his work to breeding Miniatures, and not content with that, to changing them into Moss roses and Climbers. His achievement in making them mossy is one of the most remarkable instances of taking a quality from one type of rose, and despite great difficulty, implanting it upon another. His 'Dresden Doll' is an example; and his best varieties include 'New Penny,' 'Easter Morning,' 'Judy Fischer,' and 'Rise 'n Shine.'

Louis Lens of Belgium delighted the rose world with 'Pascali'; and his 'Dame de Cœur' is a popular red Hybrid Tea in Belgium and Holland. He followed his father, Victor Lens, into the family firm in 1945, and is working to improve Hybrid Musks.

In America an organization called All-America Rose Selection plays an important part in marketing new varieties, which is always a problem to breeders, who are often better rosarians than salesmen. Robert Lindquist and O.L. Weeks are currently successful in breeding American garden roses. France appears to be full of rose breeders, among whom Georges Delbard of Paris, of the firm Delbard-Chabert, has set a high standard. His 'Vol de Nuit,' a large lilac-pink Hybrid Tea, is much admired in France, Australia, and the United States; his beautiful single red climber, 'Altissimo,' is esteemed in Britain. J. Laperrière, of the Rhône district, will long be remembered for the red HT 'Mme Louis Laperrière.'

All kinds of countries have their rose breeders and rose societies, from Poland and Czechoslovakia to South Africa and India. Their productions may be confined to their own

Ralph Moore has created many Miniatures in California.

'Pascali,' one of the greatest white Hybrid Teas: Lens, 1963.

Georges Delbard proves that not all great French rose breeders are called Meilland.

Susumu Onodera, an important Japanese breeder.

'Wendy Cussons,' rose-red Hybrid Tea, introduced by Walter Gregory in 1959.

E. F. Allen is one of the more successful of the British amateur breeders.

localities, but anything of outstanding novelty is eagerly welcomed by the international fraternity of rosarians. An example is the prostrate 'Nozomi,' which means hope; it is like a climbing white Miniature, with small single flowers in summer, and is used as a ground cover rose. It came from the Japanese hybridist Susumu S. Onodera, one of a number of able breeders in that country.

British breeders are still arising to follow the example of Henry Bennett. In 1953, Walter Gregory, of the family firm of rose growers in Nottingham, started a modest breeding station, from which came the notable successes of the rose red Hybrid Tea 'Wendy Cussons' and the climber 'Pink Perpetue.' His acknowledged intention was to try and raise some new roses for his own firm to introduce, instead of going to Holland to buy new varieties from other breeders. The present author differed from most breeders described here, by initiating rose breeding at his family firm of R. Harkness and Company, in Hertfordshire; although he is the fourth generation, the previous members of the family had not embarked on the venture. The start was made in 1962, and for some years the scale has been 2,000 crosses a year upon average. The most acceptable of his varieties, judging by their reception, are the vermilion Hybrid Tea 'Alexander,' the climber 'Compassion,' and the apricot orange Floribunda 'Southampton.'

In addition to these and other breeders, of whom many breed as a pleasurable hobby within their nursery business, there is a large and growing band of amateurs, who make a serious study of their hobby. Associations of them exist in the United States, Britain, and New Zealand. They have the example of the late Albert Norman to follow, he being as it were their patron saint as the raiser of 'Ena Harkness.' Amateurs have made some notable contributions to the rose world. 'Golden Chersonese,' raised by E.F. Allen in England, a beautiful hybrid of R. ecae, is one of the finest shrubs in existence.

Amateur or professional, breeders provide the stock in trade of the rose world; they need and deserve adequate funds to prosecute their researches.

Meanwhile most of them continue breeding out of love for a job which never has and never will earn them an adequate living. As Pat Dickson said, "Once I had started, I could not give it up."

The white 'Nozomi,' a creation of S. Onodera.

Walter Gregory of England.

'Golden Chersonese,' an Ecae Hybrid introduced in 1969 by E. F. Allen.

93

Madame
Hardy

Mme Pierre Oger  95

94   Zéphirine Drouhin

Souvenir de la Malmaison   96

97   Chapeau de Napoléon

98   Rosa Farreri Persetosa

Golden Chersonese   99

124

100   Rosa Foetida

101   Rosa Ecae

Frühlingsgold

Rosa Spinosissima Hispida

104 Rosa Foetida Bicolor

105 Golden Wings

127

106 Marguerite Hilling

107 Maigold

108 Stanwell Perpetual

109 Nevada

Celestial 111

110 Complicata

Canary Bird 112

130

113 Rosa Sericea Pteracantha

114   Lady Penzance

Fritz Nobis   115

132

116 Rosa Rubrifolia

117 Rosa Virginiana

133

Fru Dagmar Hastrup

Rosa X Pruhoniciana

120 Geranium

121 Rosa Rugosa Alba

122   Scabrosa

Roseraie de l'Hay   123

93

MADAME HARDY

Damask

Typical of a Damask rose, for its open, arching growth and pale leaves; Damasks were nearly all pale in color, and 'Madame Hardy' is white as can be. The flowers are very double, with several circles of petals laid open flat, with the tips of each row prettily displayed. There are no stamens, but a little tuft of green in the center of the flower. The fairly large, fragrant flowers are easily shattered in rough weather. The plants are tall, and may need some support; otherwise the arching shoots can thrash about in the wind. The flowers appear only once in the season, in summer.
This lovely old rose was raised in Paris at the Luxembourg Gardens and introduced in 1832.
It is named after the wife of the director of those gardens. With so much charm in the individual bloom, it looks as if Madame Hardy got a memorial that will last another century or more.

94

ZÉPHIRINE DROUHIN

Bourbon

This much loved climbing rose unfolds its deep pink flowers on many a wall about the world. The flowers are medium size or rather smaller, bright carmine pink. Although semi-double, they have enough petals to form a little quartered heart before they open. The scent is pleasant.
A great attraction of this rose is that it has scarcely any thorns. The leaves are matt, with some bronze color when young.
'Zéphirine Drouhin' flowers abundantly in summer, with some scattered bloom later in the year.
It was raised in France by Monsieur Bizot and introduced in 1868.
Little did Monsieur Bizot know that many years later, his thornless rose would be the hinge of a plot in one of Agatha Christie's detective stories. Of Monsieur Bizot himself, little is known. A light pink sport of 'Zéphirine Drouhin' was introduced in 1919 as 'Kathleen Harrop.'

95

Mme PIERRE OGER

Bourbon

The outer petals form a shallow bowl, which contains the smaller inner petals, the whole a mixture of pink and cream, very delicate and silky. The bushes are upright, somewhat lanky, fairly tall, flowering summer and autumn.
The rose is memorable for the perfection of an occasional flower, as a kind of rosy emblem of Victoriana. It is moderately fragrant. As a garden plant it has some failings, the worst being a tendency to get blackspot.
It arose in France as a sport, that is, a chance mutation, of 'Reine Victoria.' The finder was A. Oger, and his rose was introduced in 1878.
By the time this Bourbon rose came out, the class was well on the way to being supplanted by its own progeny, the Hybrid Perpetuals. There were hundreds of Bourbon roses introduced, but only a small part of them remain today. The survivors have distinctive flowers.

96

SOUVENIR DE LA MALMAISON

Bourbon

This old rose could very nearly pass for a Hybrid Tea, but frequently shows its generation in the quartered form of its large double flowers. They are light pink when young, and white when fully open. The perfume is sweet. The synonym 'Queen of Beauty and Fragrance' should not be dismissed, for the rose deserves that name.

The bushes are short in growth and free with flower; the later blooms arrive irregularly, not in a distinct second flush in the modern manner.

This lovely Bourbon was raised in France by Jean Beluze from seed of 'Mme Desprez' and introduced in 1843. Malmaison was the rose garden of the Empress Joséphine, wife for a time of Napoleon.

She assembled a great collection of roses at Malmaison, and from her garden the renowned painter of roses, Pierre Joseph Redouté, obtained his subjects.

97

CHAPEAU DE NAPOLÉON syn CRESTED MOSS

Centifolia

Remarkable for the little green extensions which surmount the buds like cockades, or as some genius put it, Napoleon's hats. They grow from the green sepals which enclose the young buds. No doubt it is much the same growth process as causes Moss roses, most of which are also Centifolias, the best being the pink 'Common Moss.'

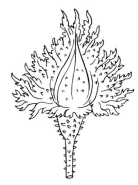

The pink flowers are double, fairly fragrant, not so interesting as their buds. The rose is not remontant, flowering only in summer. It was found in Switzerland and sent to France, where it was introduced by Vibert in 1827.

98

R. FARRERI PERSETOSA

Pimpinellifoliae

Because of the small size of the flowers, this was known for years in Britain as the Threepenny-bit Rose, after the smallest coin then in currency. It is a tall plant, over head high, with thick stems, densely covered with bristles; by contrast, its leaves and flowers would look more at home on a Miniature.

The flowers are bright pink, just five small petals surrounding bright yellow stamens; they appear in an airy manner in the summer. It is a most interesting plant, very pleasant to own; it needs more space than most.

It was raised in England from seed sent home from China by Reginald Farrer in 1914.

By growing a few roses of unusual nature, one appreciates the extraordinary diversity of the genus. The lesson to breeders is that the qualities of roses are far from being explored. Fascinating possibilities exist for the future.

99

GOLDEN CHERSONESE

Ecae Hybrid

One of the most beautiful shrubs any garden can admit. Its method of flowering is as described for *R. ecae.* The flowers are small, but larger than those of *R. ecae.* of five petals, brilliant yellow. The bushes are tall, well proportioned, with the stems angled upward, pointing their yellow-clad arms to the sky and emitting sighs of fragrance.

It is a marvelous sight in late spring for two or three weeks, after which the plants are handsome in leaf for the rest of summer.

It was raised in England by Edward F. Allen from *R. ecae* × 'Canary Bird' and introduced in 1969.

Mr. Allen is the Honorable Scientific Adviser to the Royal National Rose Society and was President in 1976, the centenary year. He has a wide knowledge of horticulture, including experience in tropical countries. He has at home in Suffolk a sister seedling of 'Golden Chersonese,' never distributed; it is of less upright habit.

100

R. FOETIDA
syn AUSTRIAN YELLOW
Pimpinellifoliae

Clear yellow flowers of five petals, borne in summer only, on shrubs about chest high. It used to be called *R. lutea* for being yellow, and has its present name for its scent, which in fact is quite pleasant. This rose has a long and vague history. It appears to have been grown from time immemorial in Persia, and in the neighboring countries from Afghanistan to Turkey. It had arrived in Europe by the late 1500s.

Naturally it was highly prized in the centuries when, with one or two relatives, it was the only bright yellow rose in cultivation.

It certainly did not originate in Austria, but most likely was first imported from Turkey into Vienna, and from there disseminated through Europe. It is not certain of being a wild rose, because it bears few seeds. It was known in Britain as the Yellow Sweet Briar; and the term 'Austrian Briar' persists.

101

R. ECAE
Pimpinellifoliae

A wild rose from Afghanistan and northwestward. It is brilliant yellow, with small flowers of five petals spangled along the branches in late spring. There are several lovely roses which share this habit of growing and flowering: the new branches which grow this year do not flower until next year; then they produce flowers along themselves, not terminally as most roses do; and each flower has a very short stalk, almost as if yellow buttons were sewn on a slim cane. Therefore these roses are not pruned in the ordinary way, because to shorten them is to take off their flowering wood. It is best to cut out some of the oldest branches, perhaps once in four years.

R. ecae is tall and open; fragrant; not remontant. Its leaves are ferny, small, divided into about 11 leaflets.

It was discovered by Dr. J. E. T. Aitchison and introduced in 1880.

102

FRÜHLINGSGOLD
Spinosissima Hybrid

This was the result of an intention to breed very hardy roses, which would thrive in northern Europe; and the method employed was to make parents of Siberian roses, whose hardiness was assumed to be beyond question. 'Frühlingsgold' is a large shrub, the size of a small tree, festooned with semi-double creamy yellow flowers in early summer. The blooms are large and fragrant, and the bushes are a rare sight when crowded with them. The foliage is tough and attractive, the plant good-looking.

It was raised in Germany by Wilhelm Kordes from 'Joanna Hill' × *R. spinosissima hispida* and introduced in 1937. The American introduction was by Bobbink and Atkins of New Jersey in 1951.

This rose needs plenty of space, and if pruned hard, or trimmed like a hedge, it will not flower freely the following year. Old parts of the plant should be removed when obvious.

103

R. SPINOSISSIMA
HISPIDA
Pimpinellifoliae

This variety of the Scotch rose grows wild in Central Asia, including Siberia. It is an extremely attractive shrub on account of its large black hips, shiny and round; the creamy yellow flowers that precede them are not without their beauty too. They are fairly large for a wild rose, and appear early in summer. The plant is large and vigorous, over head high and wider still. A fine shrub for those who have room for it. It was on record as being in cultivation in 1781, but we do not know when it first came to Europe.

Although this is considered a variety of the Scotch rose, it is different in growth, being a fine, open, upstanding shrub; whereas the Scotch rose itself is short and dense. 'Hispida' should be allowed to spread itself, for it will not give so good a display if it is trimmed short. Pruning consists of taking out old wood every three or four years.

104

R. FOETIDA BICOLOR
syn AUSTRIAN COPPER

Pimpinellifoliae

Similar to *R. foetida* in every respect, except for the flaming color of the flowers. They are vivid nasturtium-orange inside the petals, yellow without, incredibly brilliant. A shrub in full bloom is a fiery sight. However, it only lasts about two weeks in summer, and for the rest of the year is not a particularly handsome shrub.

The same mysteries apply here as to 'Austrian Yellow.' We do not know the origin, neither method nor time nor place. The reference to Austria is almost certainly because it went there from Turkey, and thence to the west.

It is certainly a sport of 'Austrian Yellow,' because it will revert to the yellow form; sometimes one branch of the bush will be yellow. Although it is often given credit for having brought the flame colors into modern roses, the main agent employed was not this rose, but 'Persian Yellow.' No doubt the two are related.

105

GOLDEN WINGS

Spinosissima Hybrid

A garden shrub of great beauty, with the advantage of being strongly remontant. Upon a bush like a shrubby Floribunda, about chest high, it bears flowers of five petals. Single they may be, but wide as one's hand. Those five petals are creamy and are ringed around a center of orange-yellow stamens and pistils. The effect is riveting. With so formidable an eye, a flower of 'Golden Wings' commands surrender from a distance. Embellished with only two or three of them, the bush becomes a spectacle.

It is incredible that any nursery should fail to stock 'Golden Wings'; it would be wasteful to plant it by the bed, since two or three plants are plenty for the average garden. There is only light fragrance.

It was raised in the United States by Roy Shepherd from 'Soeur Thérèse' × Seedling and introduced in 1956.

One of the truly great roses, a plantsman's shrub.

106

MARGUERITE HILLING

Spinosissima Hybrid

One of the world's most beautiful shrubs. It will grow head high or more, and stretches out as far; the gardener who trusts 'Marguerite Hilling' is rewarded by a profusion of large pink blooms. These have only about ten petals, but stretch them out flat, each flower covering a wide area, so that in accommodating themselves, they seem to swell the dimensions of every branch. They perch everywhere, hiding all the leaves and stems beneath them. The moderate scent gains strength by sheer numbers.

The color is like a broken pink, as if it is dappled upon white. The leaves are soft, pale, and matt, a weak point of the variety. The stems are dark, with few thorns, and the few hips are black. A summer rose, but with some flowers in the fall.

It is a sport of 'Nevada,' found in England and introduced by Thomas Hilling and Company in 1959.

107

MAIGOLD

Spinosissima Hybrid

This beautiful climbing rose has yellow flowers with a delightful touch of bronze in them. It is a wonderful climber, especially on a wall, because from an early age it will cover itself in blossom once every year, early in summer. The flowers may be a bit shaggy on close inspection, but they are fairly large, with about 14 petals, and the effect they give is inspiring. They also have a pleasant briar-like fragrance.

Some people grow 'Maigold' as a shrub, which can be done, although it is always liable to send a long shoot up in the air. Its leaves are handsome, lustrous but tough, and with the bristly stems give the impression of a plant of great character.

It was raised by Wilhelm Kordes in Germany from 'Poulsen's Pink' × 'Frühlingstag' and introduced in 1953.

Hardy; it beats most climbers in being a handsome plant while still young.

108

STANWELL PERPETUAL

Spinosissima Hybrid

This is a short little bush, with blush flowers like a Damask rose. They are double, and fairly large for the size of the plant, having dozens of petals, many of them narrow. Being a cross between Damask and Scotch, with the advantage of being remontant, 'Stanwell Perpetual' has been regarded as a little treasure for over a century.

The growth, though short, is apt to include shoots which suddenly arch up on their own. The autumn flower is usually better than the summer, blushing a little more. Two or three of these flowers in a little vase, with a sprig or two of the grayish green foliage, and a lovely Victorian picture has been made, with fragrance too.

It was raised in England by Mr. Lee from 'Quatre Saisons' × *R. spinosissima* according to the records and was introduced in 1838.

If Mr. Lee could return to his nursery, he would find himself at London Airport.

109

NEVADA

Spinosissima Hybrid

All that was written for 'Marguerite Hilling' applies equally to 'Nevada,' except for its origin and color; for 'Nevada' is white as snow. One effect of this is to render its yellow stamens more noticeable. Both roses are at their best in early summer. They produce flowers in autumn, but not nearly so liberally. 'Nevada' was raised in Spain by Pedro Dot from seed of 'La Giralda.' It was introduced in 1927. For the attribution as *Spinosissima Hybrid*, those interested are referred to *Roses*, Jack Harkness, 1978.

This will grow into a large shrub, more than head high, and arches wider still. In full bloom, it is unforgettable, purity and abundance being equal causes of wonder. It will stand clipping or shortening better than many shrub roses, but is best left alone, apart from the removal of old branches every three or four years. The small soft leaves are liable to blackspot.

110

COMPLICATA

Macrantha

Frequently listed as 'Gallica complicata,' this is a ranging shrub or semi-climber with single (five-petaled) pink flowers of great regularity of form, and consequently much beauty.

'Complicata' may be grown as a shrub, and will make quite a mound of a plant; and if given half a chance it will send long growths to rest upon the plants nearby. The flowers are fairly large for a single rose, clear pink with a light center, freely borne in summer only.

The origin of this is not known. It is clear from its description that it is ideal for a fairly wild garden or for natural sort of shrubbery.

Despite being catalogued as *R. gallica complicata*, it has very little in common with Gallicas. Rather, it is more akin to *R. X macrantha*, a blush rose found in France in 1823, with a habit like a blackberry, and no clue of its origin, apart from guesses.

111

CELESTIAL

Alba

As a class, the Albas were favorite garden roses of long ago; they are strong, long-lived shrubs, nearly all white, or slightly blush pink. Although a pale color, 'Celestial' is one of the deepest of its class, a delicate blush of light rose pink. The flowers are double, with about 27 petals, opening to medium size or smaller, holding a very beautiful shape and pure color as they show their stamens.

The bold shrub is about head high and spreads as far, with attractive, tough foliage, slightly gray-green. The scent is pleasant, perhaps not as strong as one would expect. The flowers appear only in summer.

Of uncertain origin; it is probably 200 years old, and may be older.

Albas, Damasks, and Gallicas are the genuine old-fashioned roses, so far as western record go; they were being grown in the seventeenth century. Fresh varieties came, but the line may go back to Homer.

112

CANARY BIRD

Xanthina Hybrid

This is one of the beautiful yellow roses, whose nature was described under *R. ecae.* 'Canary Bird' grows about head high and spreads wide, its ferny leaves covering the bush right down to the ground. The flowers, of five petals, appear in early summer, a lovely load of light yellow carried along the branches, causing them to arch slightly downward.
The flowers, although fairly small compared with most garden roses, are larger than those of *R. ecae* and 'Golden Chersonese.' The color is paler, and the growth less upright than in those two. Every garden should have one of these glorious heralds of the rose season; either 'Golden Chersonese' or 'Canary Bird' being the best.
The origin is uncertain, because it was mistakenly distributed as a wild rose at some time subsequent to 1907. The original *R. xanthina* comes from the Orient—north China and Korea.

113

R. SERICEA PTERACANTHA

Pimpinellifoliae

Roses have all kinds of hidden surprises, and we now meet one having enormous thorns. So large are these thorns that the base where they are joined to the stem frequently measures more than two centimeters. The thorn arises from the base as a thin, membranous growth, shaped like the sail of a ship with a sharp tip. When these thorns are young, they are red and almost translucent. The beauty of this rose is therefore in its young growth, and it may freely be cut back to encourage such growth.
The leaves are ferny and handsome, but the flowers are of slight interest, apart from having four petals, which is unusual in a rose. They are white and transient. The shrub will grow large, more than head high, and wide too.
It is a wild plant from western China and the Himalayas, introduced in 1890.
Previously *R. omeiensis.*

114

LADY PENZANCE

Eglanteria Hybrid

This rose is grown for the scent of its foliage; the famous Sweet Briar aroma arises from the leaves after rain, to pervade the garden with a refreshing scent, like pungent and delicious apples. One plant is enough to perform this service for a small modern garden, and it can be planted in an unimportant corner, for there is no great floral beauty to it; the flowers are very small, with five petals, prawn-pink touched yellow, come and gone almost before one notices them.
The growth is fairly upright, about head high; it can be trimmed to stay within bounds, for all that is needed of it is leaves.
It was raised in England by Lord Penzance from *R. eglanteria* × *R. foetida bicolor,* that is, the wild Sweet Briar × 'Austrian Copper.' It was introduced in 1894, one of a series of Sweet Briars, their names often from Scott's novels: e. g. Amy Robsart, Julia Mannering, Meg Merrilies.

115

FRITZ NOBIS

Eglanteria Hybrid

A beautiful shrub, ornament for any garden requiring a plant at least head high, and equally wide, to fill its space with an impeccable flower arrangement for two or three weeks in the summer.
The flowers are double, above medium size, and of superior shape, their petals opening in slightly crinkled circles around the center, a habit most effective. The color is pink, described by most experts as salmon-pink, but to my eyes silvery rose. The fragrance is agreeable; this plant is one of the most handsome shrubs in existence.
It was raised in Germany by Wilhelm Kordes from 'Joanna Hill' × 'Magnifica' and introduced in 1940. The two parents used by Kordes were a Hybrid Tea and a Sweet Briar, an unusual mixture. The Hybrid Tea, in improving the Briar leaves, took away their scent; but it gave fantastic beauty to the flowers. Win back scent, Mr. Breeder!

116

R. RUBRIFOLIA

Caninae

A rose to grow for its leaves, which are astounding to a stranger among roses, being covered with a purplish-gray bloom, and looking almost purple-red on the plants. They are very popular for inserting in floral arrangements. The shrub grows head high or more, and is upright, narrow for its height, bears few thorns. The flowers appear in summer, as close clusters of many little pink blossoms, of five petals. They are followed by a generous autumn show of bright red hips. This rose does not mind some shade, and more than most it needs well-drained soil.

It is a wild rose from Europe, being distributed approximately from the Pyrenees to Yugoslavia, in hilly districts. It is also known as *R. glauca* and *R. ferruginea*. The English rosarian Gordon Edwards used to advise that it be surrounded with barbed wire, to deter flower arrangers!

117

R. VIRGINIANA

Carolinae

A splendid wild rose to plant as a shrub or hedge. It has many bright leaves, furnishing the plants to the ground; and against them the bright pink flowers shine beautifully. They have five petals, and are fairly large for a wild rose. In the autumn, the leaves take on red and yellow and a generous bonus is added in the way of red hips. The plants grow about chest high, and spread as wide or more, with a kindly soft outline. They flower in summer, after most wild roses, and may have a few incidental blooms later. *R. virginiana* is a wild plant of eastern North America, especially from Newfoundland to New York and Pennsylvania.

The section to which it belongs, the Carolinae, consists of only seven species, all natives of North America exclusively, as though they were descended from an evolutionary prototype that arose in that continent, and were not found elsewhere.

118

FRAU DAGMAR HARTOPP

Rugosa Hybrid

A beautiful and healthy plant, which keeps fairly low and spreads out wide. The flowers are soft, delicate pink with yellow stamens; they have five large petals, making quite a large bloom. They appear for a long time through summer and early autumn, and are quickly followed by large red hips.

With sweet scent, and healthy Rugosa foliage, this is a valuable garden rose, long-lived and hardy. Little is recorded about its origin, but the date 1914 is associated with it, and it is presumed to be Danish. As mentioned under *Rugosa alba*, the Danes grow plenty of Rugosas, and use them as hedges. Some of the country homesteads are gone, but the Rugosas remain, and spread by suckers, so that many people think they are wild roses. Rugosas are easily grown from seed, and no doubt that is how a Dane raised this rose, for the seedlings are sure to contain variations.

119

R. X PRUHONICIANA

Moyesii Hybrid

After the same style as 'Geranium,' but with darker red flowers and a more soaring, open habit of growth. 'Geranium' is a reasonably compact shrub, although taller than a person; this goes higher, and then arches out wider. The flowers and hips have the same rare and wonderful beauty already described in 'Geranium.' These gifts come from the Chinese *R. moyesii*, and should be seen by everyone who wishes to appreciate the wonders of roses.

This hybrid's origin is not perfectly clear; it was obtained about 1920. I believe it may have come from Czechoslovakia, for there is a place near Prague called Průhonice, where the Botanical Garden of the Czechoslovak Academy of Sciences is situated. Presumably they raised this rose from seed of *R. moyesii*, as the Royal Horticultural Society did with 'Geranium.' The Czech garden now boasts almost one thousand varieties.

120

GERANIUM

Moyesii Hybrid

A large shrub, which has some extraordinary beauties to unfold, to the wonder of anyone who never saw it before. First, the scarlet flowers, of a bright yet dusky red, lit by a precisely ordered ring of dusty yellow stamens, the whole as exact as a heraldic symbol straight from the drawing board.

Then, in autumn, the long hips hang down, from day to day ripening to a shining red, until they present as remarkable a picture as the versatile genus *Rosa* affords, a combination of rich color and graceful lines.

'Geranium' was raised in England from *R. moyesii* in the Royal Horticultural Society's gardens and was introduced in 1938. *R. moyesii* itself is a wild rose from southwest China. 'Geranium' is compact compared with *R. moyesii*, which sends long shoots soaring into the air like fishing rods. Another rose with similar hips, but fewer thorns, is *R. macrophylla*.

121

R. RUGOSA ALBA

Cinnamomeae

The Rugosa roses are a distinct section of the genus. They are chiefly marked by their thick leaves: wrinkled and shiny green above, softly pale and downy below, and highly resistant as a rule to diseases. The flowers are broad for wild roses, and continue to flower for a long period. *R. rugosa alba* has flowers of five petals, very clean-cut, with attractive yellow stamens. The flowers are fragrant, produced from early to late summer, and succeeded by bright red, rounded hips. The plants grow up to chest high, spread out fairly wide, and are very hardy. The stems are closely set with thin thorns like bristles.

The original species is pink, and grows wild chiefly in coastal districts in China, Korea, north Japan, and east Russia; it came to Europe about 1845; for this white form we have no date.

Visitors to Denmark admire lovely white and purple Rugosas.

122

SCABROSA

Rugosa Hybrid

One of the finest shrubs, with its superbly healthy Rugosa leaves, and large flowers of five petals blooming from early summer and into autumn. Their size, for single flowers, is large; and the mauve red color is quite dramatic, especially when it is young and dark, with the pale dusty stamens glowing like a torch bulb in the center. The fragrance is rich, and the hips bright red and fat. The plant grows head high and spreads wide. It can make a wonderful hedge, partly because its lower shoots are just sufficiently lax to sweep the ground and cover the plant from head to foot.

Its origin is uncertain; it was discovered in England on the author's family nursery, but nobody knows how it got there. Instead of choosing a nice name for it, we entrusted the experts to identify it, with what I shall always consider an unfortunate result. The meaning of the name is "rough."

123

ROSERAIE DE L'HAŸ

Rugosa Hybrid

Bright purple flowers are backed by light green leaves, on shrubs about head high. That description conceals a rose of extraordinary color, very bold and handsome, with large double flowers, loosely formed. It can make a startling and definite hedge. The flowers are pleasantly fragrant, the foliage of excellent Rugosa type. The flowering time is summer, and continuing late with abated zeal. There are no hips.

This was raised in France by Cochet-Cochet and introduced in 1902. The parentage is not known for certain.

The name is that of a famous rose garden in Paris, started by Jules Gravereaux, and given to the city in 1893. The speciality of the garden is a collection of old roses, the original idea having been to assemble all those once possessed by the Empress Joséphine. Monsieur Gravereaux owned the famous store Bon Marché.

HOW TO GROW ROSES

THE BASIC STEPS

1. Choose a site with sunlight, drainage, wind shelter.

2. Prepare the soil. Keep topsoil at the top. Apply humus materials and minerals as necessary; let resettle.

3. Measure out the plant locations, dig shallow holes, plant roots firmly in the ground.

4. General cultivation: Kill weeds, remove suckers, secure ties and stakes, keep soil hoed. Perform maintenance.

5. Feed roses at prescribed times with manures and fertilizers.

6. Health care: Prevent pests and predators, and fight persistent enemies with sprays.

7. During dormant seasons, prune the branches as necessary for good growth.

The golden rule of successful rose-growing is to imitate, as much as possible, the natural conditions in which roses have prospered for so many centuries. Growing roses is not difficult; the rewards—as seen here with the exuberant shrub 'Fashion'—are considerable.

This chapter deals with care and cultivating of roses. For advice on garden planning, landscaping, and arranging, see "Enjoying Your Roses," pages 73–88.

The first thing to understand about growing roses is that it is very easy, provided the environment is naturally to the rose's liking. Most of the printed instructions are designed to struggle against bad environments; or else to teach the gardener to undo the harm he ought not to have done. Nothing, surely, could be simpler than planting a root in the ground, and letting it grow.

The rose grower's syllabus contains seven simple subjects:

The Site, to place the plant where it can grow.
The Soil, to provide the means of sustaining growth.
Planting, to start the plant's life in a prosperous way.
Cultivating, to guide it to flower perfectly.
Feeding, to imitate a perfect environment.
Health, to preserve it from pests and diseases.
Pruning, that its strength is saved from dissipation.

By considering each of these subjects in turn, a short, simple, and comprehensive guide can be given to rose growing. But in order to tear away the blindfold and see, the reader should study *why* more closely than *how;* horticulture is no more an exact science than is bringing up children. By knowing the reason for an operation, the rose grower learns to adjust that operation to the needs of individual plants. Thus he may understand a rose and its life-style.

THE SITE

Roses are descended from wild plants which adapted them-selves to live in particular environments. Unless their place in cultivation successfully imitates their natural haunts, they will be in much the same case as a fish in a tree, which can only be kept alive by taking an aquarium up a ladder.

WHERE TO PLANT YOUR ROSES

A sunny site: The cooler your cli-mate, the less shade your roses will want.

A dry site: Where water and rain will drain away, not leav-ing roots waterlogged.

A sheltered site: Some protection in excessively windy places.

Their natural element was in temperate regions; therefore in colder climates they may require protection in the winter, and in tropic climates protection, such as filtered shade, from the sun.

Most of them naturally grew as shrubs among low vege-tation, and their object was to place their leaves in the sun. Therefore, in temperate or cold regions, they must be planted in a sunny place. They have some tolerance of shade, up to about half the day.

All roses, except for a few American species, are dry land plants. They like the rain to descend, percolate, and drain away. Therefore it is useless to plant them in ground where their roots will be regularly sitting in water. Such a plot would need to be drained, or else raised.

Most roses lived naturally in colonies, that is, in a group of rose shrubs, with various other plants intruding. They got some shelter from the wind thereby. But if wind is incessant, or violent, or very cold, it becomes a danger.

THE SOIL

The soil is first of all an anchor to plants, and secondly a kind of living sponge, from which they may absorb its various minerals dissolved in water. Both condition of the soil and its ingredients are to be clearly understood as being essentials, of equal importance.

The condition is a matter of management by cultivation, best achieved before the roses are planted. To understand what is wanted, bear in mind that the roots must be held so firmly as to resist any forces the wind may blast at the superstructure; and consider the nature of a rose root.

The root starts to grow in the spring, soft, white, and thin, and is supplied with an emollient to help it ease its way into the hard soil encountered in nature. Thus, from the start, it expects to live in soil pressure, which obviously increases as the root matures and thickens. It absorbs moisture through pores in its skin; it therefore requires soil around its skin, not a large hole of air.

To provide those conditions, the cultivator must ensure that either by his tools, or by frost, or by time, the soil is broken fine, and resettled into the various air pockets made by cultivation. Then he may plant his roses.

The corollary is that he should not subsequently disturb the soil around the roots by digging deeply among his roses. He should also avoid compacting the surface of the soil by constantly walking upon it. The top thumb depth should be loose, and all soil under it firm: that is comfort to roses, their natural floor.

The ingredients of the soil are not easily determined; and if some items are deficient, they can usually be added. Essential ingredients must not only be present, but also available to the plant—and it is this point which may render a soil analysis misleading. The ingredients are water, humus, and minerals.

Water, as already stated, should descend, percolate, and drain away. In very dry areas, it will be found necessary to supply it, and if it is likely to be permanently necessary, a trickle irrigation system is recommended. In many cases water will be required only in very dry spells, when transpiration from the foliage exceeds intake and the leaves respond by hanging down instead of looking to the sky. Water on the plants in the evening will then transform them magically.

Humus is the evidence of life in the soil, whereby the organisms in it have multiplied in the course of disposing of the

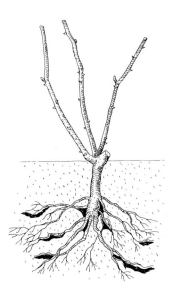

Soil must be soft and loose enough to allow roots to penetrate and grow—but not so loose that air pockets (see the blackened areas on the sketch) surround the roots.

Left: *The wild* Rosa spinosissima hispida, *a large, upstanding variety of the Scotch rose. The wild roses from which our varieties descend were quite hardy. Many were climbers or trailers which grew in the shade, with the object of thrusting their stems through bushes or trees to flower in the sun. Thus we can plant our climbers in a shady place, provided they may flower in sunlight.*

147

1. *Dig the soil as necessary, replacing each stratum in its original position.*

2. *While digging, mix humus-forming materials (such as dung or compost) into the soil for enrichment.*

3. *Difficult soils (clay, too acid, too alkaline) may be improved at digging time by certain additives.*

4. *Leave the soil to resettle before planting.*

1. Topsoil, the covering, is the fertile earth. Its depth varies considerably. In exceptional cases, the topsoil can extend quite deep, with little change of color or texture as much as 30 centimeters (12 inches) down; but most topsoil is far shallower.

2. Lower stratum. This less fertile layer will show a difference in color and will have a rougher texture than the topsoil. Humus-forming material may be mixed through these two strata; anything likely to grow (such as turf) should be placed well below the topsoil. The lower stratum should be loosened.

3. Subsoil, the third stratum. This is often hard and impenetrable by water and roots, and therefore may need to be loosened. Having removed the top two strata, one can simply plunge a strong fork into the subsoil and push it to and fro. If the subsoil is intractable clay, it can be improved by forking in gypsum (calcium sulfate), 1.5 kilos per square meter (3 1/4 pounds per square yard).

droppings from plants and animals; and in that process, the mineral contents of the soil are constantly changing, to the best possible sustenance of plant life. This is assisted by digging in as much humus-forming material as one can, broken and mixed with the soil; this must be done at the time of cultivation before planting. The obvious materials to use are dung or garden compost (both already well rotted down), leaf mold, chopped turves (upside down and deep enough to die), wood ash. Imagine what falls to the ground in nature, and one may as a rule safely incorporate it; but not woody branches, not pine needles, not pieces of heather—those items were not normally to be found in the natural territory of roses.

In the years after planting, humus-forming materials can be spread on the surface of the soil.

The necessary *minerals* may be presumed to be present if one lives either in an area where roses grow wild, or where they are being successfully cultivated by one's neighbors. Deficiencies are more usually experienced not from the absence of a mineral, but rather because it is present but unavailable. This occurs in soils which are very acid, or on the contrary very alkaline. There is a numerical scale to measure these characters, called the pH scale, which in cases of doubt may be ascertained, usually by recourse to the local representative of the government's horticultural services. The ideal pH for roses is 6.5, but their tolerance is such that they can grow well from just over 4 up to 8.

The lower the pH, the more acid the soil, and the better it is for ericaceous plants such as rhododendrons and heather. This is not a natural environment for roses, but may be improved, usually only to a limited extent, by adding lime or wood ash, and never adding peat.

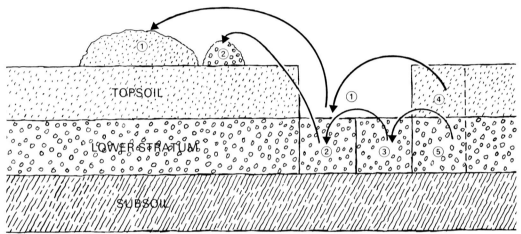

This digging scheme for loosening and enriching allows the various strata to be kept separate and re-placed at their correct depth.

1. Remove topsoil from two trenches and set aside.

2. Remove the lower stratum from the first trench and set aside. One now has access to the subsoil, so that it can be loosened as required.

3. Dig out the lower stratum from the second trench and put it in the former site of 2.

4. Dig out topsoil from the third trench and place it above 2.

5. Dig out lower stratum from third trench and place in former site of 3.

This pattern is continued until the whole plot is prepared. Finally 2 is replaced in the bottom of the final trench, and 1 is used to fill the top-soil for the last two trenches.

On the contrary, if the pH is high, then one endeavors to lower it with peat or sulfate of potash, and one shuns lime like a saint resisting temptation.

Finally, the soil needs to be of sufficient depth to anchor and sustain the roses. It is useless to plant them if the soil is so shallow that the roots rest in subsoil. (See the illustration of the three levels of soil on the opposite page.) The roots and water must be able to penetrate to a depth of some 30 centimeters (12 inches), and thus the various strata will have to be loosened and enriched to that depth. In some gardens, a depth of 30 centimeters will extend all the way into the subsoil; in others, it will reach only the lower stratum; while some few lucky gardeners will find that their topsoil goes deep enough to accommodate full root growth, without the need to cultivate the lower stratum and subsoil.

The method of digging a plot depends on the cultivation that plot needs. The working system is to remove from one end of the plot the various strata of soil to be cultivated, and dump them at the far end, in separate heaps, where they are reserved to fill in the final trench. Thus one may work in comfort, keep the surface level, and return each stratum in the same order in which it was found. If two strata are to be cultivated, then the top one will have to be removed from two trenches.

The aim to achieve when planting a rose is to place its roots firmly in well-cultivated soil, so that they may become securely fastened to the ground in the shortest possible time. The best time to plant roses with bare roots is in autumn or spring, when the soil has some warmth in it. Roses grown in containers are best planted in late spring or early summer. We are of course assuming that readers are buying rose plants ready-made from a supplier.

A plant is a live thing, and is not to be cut off from its life

For miniatures, 25 cm (10 in.) make an adequate interval.

Dwarf Floribundas (center sketch, below) require a distance of some 35 cm (14 in.) between plants.

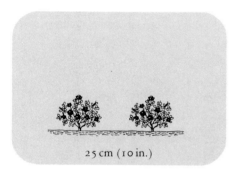

25 cm (10 in.)

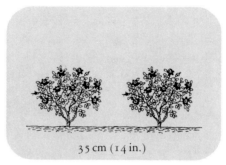

35 cm (14 in.)

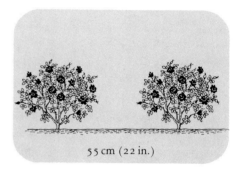

55 cm (22 in.)

Planning before planting: The ground must be staked out to allow appropriate space between rose plants. The five sketches give approximate guidelines for the various types of plants.

support system any longer than necessary. People who receive dogs, cats, or tropical fish would not dream of leaving them lying about. The same policy should apply to plants. If a number of plants is to be placed in some particular design, for example to fill a bed, then the planting positions should be marked out beforehand; short sticks or labels can serve as markers, one for each plant. It is best to cut three measuring sticks, one as a measure from the edge of the bed, and the other two at the length between the plants. These sticks can then be laid upon the ground to find where each marker should be set. Work around the perimeter of the bed first, and in the center last; adjustments can be made, for distance is not a critical factor; if major adjustments must be made, they are normally less obvious at the center than at the perimeter.

The average planting distances are as follows, but may be varied according to the luxuriance of growth experienced locally, and to the habit of individual varieties:

    Miniatures: 25 cm (10 in.)
    Dwarf Floribundas: 35 cm (14 in.)
    Normal Hybrid Teas and Floribundas: 55 cm (22 in.)
Shrub roses vary in growth too greatly to abide by a facile figure. As an approximate guide, two-thirds of the expected height is a reasonable planting distance.

The third sketch, for normal Hybrid Teas or Floribundas, indicates a space of 55 cm (22 in.) between plants—a very approximate figure. Another good rule of thumb for normal Hybrid Teas and Floribundas is to leave a distance two-thirds of the plant's expected height.

Climbing Roses: Against suitable supports; distance is immaterial, so long as it is not too close, and the intended training of the plant is borne in mind. As a general rule, anything less than 3 meters (120 in.) will be much too close.

Standard or Tree Roses: Optional; they are best placed sparsely, to give an effect of broken height. If a row of standards is required, 2 meters (80 in.) apart is satisfac-

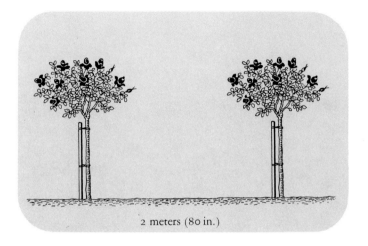

2 meters (80 in.)

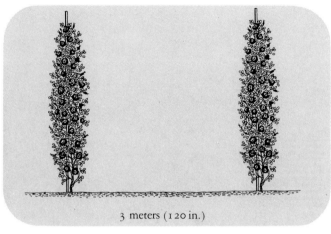

3 meters (120 in.)

Standard or Tree roses are most effective when planted rather far apart. Two meters (80 in.) is about the minimum, unless a special effect is sought.

tory; they would be set closer only if the garden picture in the owner's mind demanded it.

From the edge of the bed: For normal Hybrid Teas and Floribundas, 40 cm (16 in.); but special circumstances may apply; for example, the narrowness of a path may demand that the roses be set further back. Other types should be spaced according to their expected growth.

Most roses can be grown as specimen plants, whether singly or in groups. If space allows, a group of three or five shrub roses of the same variety can look quite magnificent. Many roses can also be grown as hedges, planted either in single or double rows. If in a single row, the planting distances can well be on the close side.

It is no use spoiling the carefully cultivated bed by trampling about on it trying to plant roses that arrived when the soil was saturated or frozen. The plants may be stored safely in cool temperatures from 1° to 5°C (34° to 41°F) for a considerable period; or even in slightly higher temperatures if they are kept humid. Wind and drafts must be avoided.

However, if they cannot be planted fairly promptly in their chosen positions, they should be temporarily planted, sharing the same trench, with their roots kept moist.

In order to plant roses firmly, it is axiomatic that the ground under the roots should not be disturbed; it has already been

Climbing roses will need some space for horizontal extension, so one should leave at least 3 meters (120 in.) between each plant.

cultivated and allowed to resettle. Therefore the depth of the hole to be dug ought to match the depth required by the roots. This is not necessarily the same as their length, because the pliable parts of the roots can with great advantage be allowed to assume a horizontal position, for thus they cover a wider area, are more easily set firmly, and are nearer to the warmth of the sun. Therefore the hole need not be as deep as most people suppose.

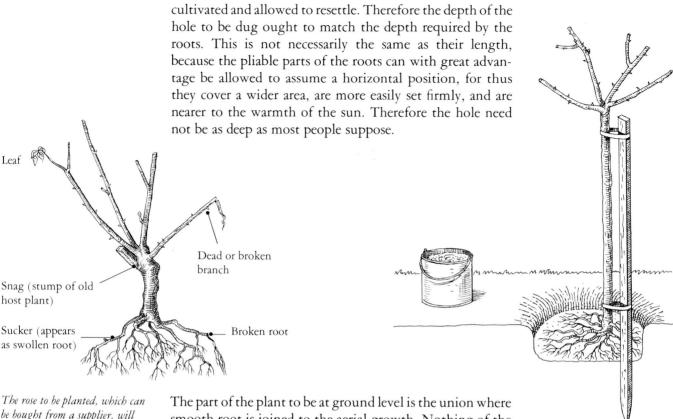

Leaf

Dead or broken branch

Snag (stump of old host plant)

Sucker (appears as swollen root)

Broken root

The rose to be planted, which can be bought from a supplier, will look approximately as shown here. Before planting, examine it carefully and remove any useless pieces or foreign bodies, as illustrated.

Stakes, essential for Standard or Tree roses, must be driven in the ground before the plant is placed in the hole. Note the length and position for the stake. Other types of roses will not require stakes.

The part of the plant to be at ground level is the union where smooth root is joined to the aerial growth. Nothing of the character of root should be exposed to the air, and very little of the character of stem should be buried in the soil. Standard (Tree) roses should be planted with as little as possible of the stem being buried.

A plant should be examined before it is planted; look for useless pieces which ought to be removed. These include broken roots, or a snag left at the union (the snag is the stump of the old host plant), or dead twigs or broken pieces of branches, or leaves, or suckers, which sometimes in their incipient state appear as a swelling on a root.

If the plant is to be staked, the stake should be driven in before the plant goes into its hole. Stakes are essential for Standard (Tree) roses, and should end just below the lower union of the rose and the standard stem. For other roses stakes are not normally necessary.

The roots should be made wet and placed in the hole, with the union at ground level. If the roots run more or less in one direction, the easiest way to place the plant is against one side of the hole. Then the union where stems and roots meet can be placed exactly at soil level. If, however, the roots are such that the plant cannot be set to one side of the hole, then it must be placed more centrally; to ensure that the union is at ground level, a stick laid across the hole from side to side would give a useful guide to an inexperienced planter. Thus, one way or the other, the plant is sitting in the hole, the lower part of its roots more or less horizontal. They should be covered with fine soil, and firmly trodden.

At this stage some people use a planting mixture, made of peat and bone meal; peat is not a good substance in acid soils, but it is helpful in alkaline soil. However, if the soil

Placing the plant in the ground: If roots run primarily in one direction, the plant can be placed against one side of the hole, as shown here. The hole is filled with earth and a peat mixture if necessary.

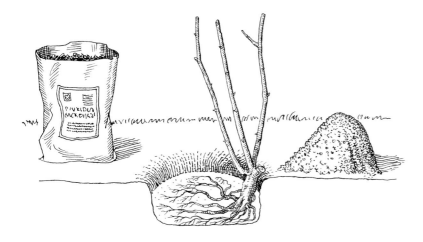

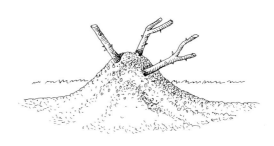

In a cold, windy, and very dry climate, part of the stem can be covered with a mound of soil for protection. Once warm weather begins, this covering is removed.

PLANTING YOUR ROSES

1. Measure and mark the position for each plant; observe proper distances.

2. Plant when soil is neither soaked nor frozen; autumn and spring are the best times.

3. Dig a hole large enough to let the plant sit upright, but with its pliable roots horizontal.

4. Check the plant and roots, removing broken or dead roots and branches; pests; suckers.

5. Moisten the roots. Place the plant upright in the hole, the pliable roots toward the horizontal at the bottom of the hole; the union between roots and shoots at ground level.

6. Cover roots with fine soil and tread on it firmly. Check that the plant sits tightly and erect.

is good a planting mixture is unnecessary; put some more soil in, and tread very firmly again, so that the hole is about two-thirds full. At this stage it is permissible to put in some well-rotted compost or manure, as an extra bonus; and then fill up with soil to agree with the level of the bed.

When planted, the rose should sit tight in the ground, and feel firm against a pull by finger and thumb.

In a climate where the weather is expected to be very dry, especially with cold winds, some soil can be drawn around the plant in a little hill to cover part of the stems. It should be removed when the weather favors the new season's growth.

The easiest way to plant is to put aside the soil from the first hole, and fill that hole with the soil from the second; fill the second hole by digging out the third, and so continue.

One particular problem is that of replacement in a bed, for which the normal prior cultivation is impossible; and worse still the soil has been used by a previous rose bush. The answer is to dig out the condemned plant as soon as possible, take out the soil it sat in, so far as may be done without disturbing its neighbors, and replace it with the best fresh soil one has on hand, preferably with well-rotted manure or compost mixed in. Leave it to settle, and then plant the replacement.

CULTIVATING

Each one of the headings in this chapter is in fact a part of the cultivation of roses; but there is an additional sense of helping them along in a general way, apart from the more clearly defined operations such as planting, pruning, feeding; and it is the miscellany of general details that we con-

Left: Even when the roses are at their peak, cultivation and regular care must continue. The grower will need to spend pleasant hours attending to a lovely bed of roses in full bloom, to remove weeds and suckers and to keep the soil hoed. Summer is, in particular, the time for removing dying blooms (if the roses are remontant, i.e. repeat-bloomers).

Right: One of the rose's enemies is the sucker, a shoot arising directly from the rootstock rather than from the stem of the plant, as in the photograph. Once a sucker has been recognized, it should be pulled out if possible. If it is too strong, one must dig down (as in the sketch) to the juncture of the sucker and the root. The sucker is then cut off flush with the root.

sider here. Most of them can be performed in a pleasant and relaxed way, as a result of regularly inspecting one's roses, and thereby forming a close acquaintanceship with them. It is one of gardening's great pleasures to find your plants are old friends.

Year-Round Care. Through the whole year, there are three tasks which should be done as soon as they are seen: to kill weeds, to remove suckers, and to secure ties.

Never make a friend of a weed, by deceiving oneself that it may have some protective value. It will repay such weakness by multiplying a thousandfold, and will prove as protective as a strangler. Either hoe it or pull it out; or if the problem is beyond manual management, kill it chemically, taking great care that the product chosen either will not harm the roses or will not come into contact with them.

The most difficult weed in many temperate countries is bindweed *(Convolvulus arvensis),* which entwines itself closely around the stems of the roses. If so found, it should be broken, leaving the long strands to die on the rose bush; the broken ends, and especially the young tips emerging from the ground, should be treated with Systemic Brush-wood Killer, taking great care not to let the killer touch the rose. Do not use a sprayer, better a paintbrush or cloth, so long as any warnings on the container are not disregarded. For bad spots close to the roses, this should be done two or three times a year, until the weed is no longer alive.

On suckers, the best advice is: If you see a sucker, take it out; it will be harder tomorrow. A sucker is a shoot arising from the root of the plant, and because roses are propagated as a rule by being budded onto the root of a wild rose, then the sucker has the nature of that root. It is part of the wild rose's survival kit, enabling it to grow after being burned or eaten to the ground.

Suckers can be recognized because their point of origin is from the rootstock, instead of from the rose budded onto it; and from a difference in appearance, which in some cases is unfortunately not always obvious without much practice. There is no easy identification by counting the leaflets, as is often but falsely supposed.

In spring and early summer, suckers can often be pulled out, but the force needed must never be so great as to disturb the roots. If pulling does not work, then a small excavation should be made to the point of origin, where the sucker should be cut out flush with the root. Leave a millimeter, and it will respond with more growth, in gratitude for the hard pruning it had. If a sucker is large and troublesome, it may be better in some cases to sacrifice the root upon which it grows, by cutting through the root each side of the sucker.

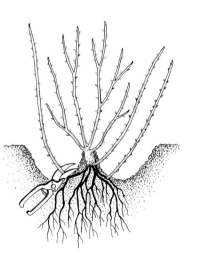

Standard (Tree) roses are budded not only upon a foreign root, but also a foreign stem, upon which suckers are liable to grow. The best way to dispose of stem suckers is to rub them off with the fingers while they are very small. This avoids cuts and scars upon the stem.

The ties of standards and of climbers should be renewed whenever they become loose, for no matter the season, there can always be a high wind next week. In the case of climbers, new shoots should be secured during the summer as they are noticed, for they are the plants' future, and their loss should not be risked. The inspection of ties is particularly to be advised in autumn and during the winter.

Through most of the year, attention should be given to cul-

GENERAL CULTIVATION: YEAR-ROUND

Keep the soil free of all weeds.

Keep the plants free of suckers.

Keep ties and stakes secure.

See also: Health Care.

tivating the topsoil when the weather is dry enough. One of the most valuable times is in the autumn, to leave it nicely hoed for winter. Then it will be much more easily dealt with in the spring; the converse is to let the sins of last summer sour during the winter, so that the reformation required in spring grows into an arduous task. Should it prove to be beyond the hoe, then a small sharp spade can be used, just to chip the ground in order to open the surface; leave the

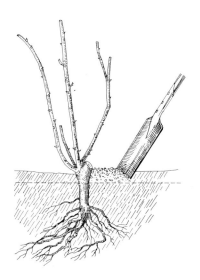

If the ground has hardened a great deal over the winter. spring hoeing may prove quite difficult. The first step in spring. then. would be to loosen up the surface soil by chipping with a small spade.

soil to experience some drying days, and then the hoe can be used.

Footprints in the rose beds should be hoed loose again; the less one walks on rose soil, the better; but it is of course unavoidable. Trouble awaits the gardener who does it when the soil is wet.

For all the hopeful efforts to garden without actually doing any work, nobody has come up with a better means than a good hoe. But when using it, or any other tool among the roses, do not hit the plants; a likely result of that carelessness is canker.

Seasonal Care. In the early spring, it is pleasant to see the first signs of growth on the roses, as the eyes awake, and stretch into little green leaves. At this time, if the plants were protected against the winter by a hill of soil or other material, remove it, so that the sun can induce growth from the base of the plant.

It may be seen that of the newly planted roses, one here and there is not growing as soon as the more lively ones. The best first aid for it is to tread it very firmly, when the soil

Rose bushes are normally cut back in autumn so that they offer a lower profile to winter winds. An exception is made for some Shrub roses (above). *which look much better in spring if long shoots have been left intact all winter long.*

is dry, in case the plant has worked loose in the ground. Then pour a bucketful of water over it; and another one if the water runs away at once. The water washes fine soil particles down to the roots.

As more and more eyes burst into growth, it may be seen that from one eye, there are occasionally two or even three little shoots arising. If the intention is to have superlative blooms, then the smaller shoots can be rubbed off with

SEASONAL CULTIVATION

Spring: Check firmness of newly planted roses. Hoe, or chip soil with a spade. Trim off stubs and pruning errors. Shorten blind or damaged roots.
See also: Planting; Feeding; Pruning.

Summer: Hoe. Disbud if desired. Remove old flowers. See also: Feeding.

Autumn: Hoe. Top growth may be shortened to prevent wind damage.
See also: Preparing the Soil; Planting; Pruning.

Winter: Remove and burn dead leaves. Apply sheltering mounds of soil or peat, if winter protection is essential.

Above right: *A rose with a double center—one of the anomalies one can sometimes encounter in the rose garden. This is of course a curiosity. rather than a deformity or a dangerous symptom.*

finger and thumb, to leave one per eye. This operation will not bother any gardener but the perfectionist, who has an eye to exhibiting his flowers.

All gardeners should survey their roses in the spring to look for stubs left after pruning. One sometimes prunes too high above an eye, or mistakes its position; or very often the designated eye has refused to grow, and a lower one has sprouted instead. With a sharp pair of secateurs, those stubs may be removed, for otherwise they are liable to be used by insects as living quarters.

Spring brings its troubles along with its promise, and most of these are considered under "Feeding" and "Health." But there are two aberrations of growth commonly found, blind shoots and distorted shoots.

A blind shoot is one where the growing point gives up growing, and usually ends just above a leaf, with no intention of proceeding upward to form a flower bud. The reasons for this are not usually clear, but they probably have some relation to the amount of light or temperature at quite an early stage of the growth. The answer is to remove the

Distorted shoots or leaves. as seen here. can result either from insects or from pesticide that has been misdirected or carried on the breeze. If these shoots are cut off in time, the plant as a whole will normally survive.

157

top of the shoot, down to a point just above a leaf, taking off probably a length of about 12 to 20 cm (5 to 8 in.).

Distorted shoots may result from the work of insects, but they can also show that some herbicide has passed through the air, and visited the plant. The atmosphere contains currents of unexpected courses and herbicides can be conducted through it in a quite unforeseen way. If the top leaves become elongated or otherwise grotesque, cut off the affected portion, to a point just above a sound leaf, and the plant will normally recover.

When the buds appear, one may try the experiment of disbudding. For ordinary garden display, it is unnecessary; but if one wishes to cut the flowers it is a sensible practice, because if one cuts the bloom the unopened buds around it are doomed anyway, and it would have been better to guide their resources elsewhere. Disbudding should be carried out when the buds are very small, just big enough to handle. If three or more good buds are close together at the top of a Hybrid Tea stem, leave the center one alone, but pull out those around it. They usually snap off, upon a gentle movement away from the perpendicular. The results of this will be to make the remaining central bud grow into a larger flower than it would otherwise have done; and also to cause side shoots lower on the stem to start growing sooner.

It is not necessary to disbud types other than Hybrid Teas or Hybrid Perpetuals. But exhibitors like to improve their Floribundas by disbudding the central bud of a cluster. That is the bud which flowers first, all on its own, in many varieties. By removing it, the cluster flowers more evenly.

Sometimes roses grow happily to the bud stage, but instead of then turning into a bloom, the bud either withers or rots. Better not waste time arguing, for the damage is done, and the shoot might as well be shortened to try again. The causes of withering are obscure, but suggest that the stem was not able to supply what was called for by the bud, when trying to grow into a flower. This could be from drought, or root disturbance, or from a wound on the stem choking the vital movement of supplies just inside the bark.

Rotting is normally from excess moisture making the petals stick, although greenfly can contribute with their stickiness. Once a flower begins to rot, some botrytis (a kind of mildew) soon grows on the petals. Apart from that after-effect, neither the withering nor the rotting is a disease, only a mechanical failure.

After the glorious flowers of summer have delighted us, they immediately turn to their proper business, which is to set

Floribundas. such as 'Queen Elizabeth' pictured here. require no disbudding. However. some growers like to remove the central. largest bud of a very large Floribunda cluster so that the buds surrounding it reach a full. even pattern. This would have to be done while all the buds are very young.

seed. This process absorbs much of the energy of the plant, and provides a disincentive to further flowering. Therefore it is well to perform the pleasant summer task of removing the old flowers as soon as they cease to please. Short pieces of stem may be cut off with them, down to a sound leaf. This practice of "deadheading" is only carried out on remontant roses to encourage the next flowers.

By autumn, these wanderings in the garden may begin to

Left: *Hybrid Tea 'National Trust' shown at its full, rich growth as the result of disbudding. The process consists of the removal of all but one bud on a stem, to concentrate energy on one flower. Disbudding is practiced primarily by exhibitors and specialists, although it can also be recommended for those who raise roses for cutting and displaying indoors.*

Deadheading—removal of blooms past their prime—is necessary in summer to prepare the way for new growth. A rose that flowers only once a season, like 'Lady Penzance' at left, does not need this care. Its surviving blooms can be left even . into autumn, when hips begin to appear.

Left:
This photograph of 'Pink Favorite' demonstrates rose growth without disbudding. The result is smaller flowers, but more of them. Hybrid Teas and Hybrid Perpetuals are the only classes that will require disbudding.

lose the glamour and the comfort of summer; and the necessity to remove old flowers is obviously past. At some time it will be obvious that the roses will not flower much more this season, but they may have a considerable amount of top growth as a possible victim of winter's winds. Then it is sensible to trim them down to a shipshape height to stand the wind, with the motive of preventing their rocking to and fro. This does not apply, however, to some of the Shrub roses, whose spring beauty is greatly increased by long, tenuous shoots, which must therefore take their chance in the winter, and do not in any case offer sufficient wind resistance as to make the plant rock.

With winter, the leaves fall; and leaves are now to be regarded as possible sanctuaries for any pest or disease seeking shelter. Therefore they should be gathered and burned. At the same time, those who live in harshly cold climates should apply their winter protection, as hillocks of dry soil, or peat, or other suitable material around the base of the plants.

Roses that were newly planted in autumn may become raised and loosened by winter frosts; if so, they should be trodden firm again, as soon as the soil is dry.

FEEDING

Roses respond to good feeding; which is another way of saying they look so much better from being fed, that anyone who does not take the trouble will be put to shame by the contrast.

One must learn what good feeding is; then, with under-

The healthy roses pictured on these pages are meant to show the fine results of proper feeding. The first step is to treat the soil, before planting, with the proper additives. Thereafter, feeding will be carried out according to particular conditions. The radiant Hybrid Tea at right is 'Silver Jubilee.'

standing, one can administer it. There is no simple recipe, because soils are different, and a good feed in one may be poison in another.

Plants are fed naturally by minerals or their compounds in the soil; the stock of minerals is maintained and made available by the decomposition of the remains of plants and animals. This decomposition has two major effects: first, it releases and compounds the minerals in a manner to make them readily received; and second, it improves the texture and efficiency of the soil thanks to the enormous multiplication of its living organisms.

Plants may also be fed artificially by adding minerals as a kind of medicine ready to be taken; this is the purpose of the rose fertilizers sold in gardening shops.

Both methods have their value, and can be used together.

Organic Manuring. The natural method is known as organic manuring, and it is a copy of nature's method of disposing of both animal and vegetable matter. The mixture is important; animal and vegetable residues should both be present, for they help to digest one another.

The best animal residue is farmyard manure, which receives its vegetable content from straw; alternatives are shoddy (waste from wool) and fish. Those items have bulk; more concentrated are dried blood, bone meal, and hoof and horn, these being the powdered remains of waste animal products. The best vegetable residue is well-made garden compost, which receives some animal content in its making. Alternatives are wood ash, leaf mold, young green plants, and chopped turf. All these are bulky. Leaf mold is best avoided in the more excessively acid or alkaline soils.

As natural products are not always easily available in modern cities, there are certain manufactured substitutes. Bulky ones are in the form of composts, often containing soil, or dung, or vegetable materials; and there are many based on peat, with some animal content, commonly sewage. Sewage itself is also reconstituted for garden use, but should be checked to ensure it does not contain too high a proportion of such waste-pipe minerals as lead or zinc, which can be injurious to plants. Concentrated, nonbulky products are made from seaweed and from the waste products of fish and many other materials.

Remembering that whichever of these substances is chosen, there should be a combination of animal and vegetable, the gardener may incorporate his choice in the soil when preparing his rose beds.

Thereafter the good work may continue through the years after the roses have been planted, by spreading bulky humus-forming materials on the surface of the ground; but do not of course use any green plants likely to root or seed. Material should be applied in the spring, when the soil has lost its winter chill, and before the plants have grown large again after being pruned. If well-rotted farmyard manure is used, it is helpful to sift some fine peat or soil over it, to prevent the nitrogen escaping into the air; and the same practice will be helpful with young green plants.

If bulky material is not available, then the products of blood, bone, hoof and horn, or seaweed may be used instead, usually at about 125 grams to the square meter (4 ounces per square yard) but having regard to the instructions given with the product concerned; these may vary according to the additives inserted by the manufacturer. Bone meal and hoof and horn work slowly, and should be applied early.

Pink and yellow 'Peace.' Although prime feeding time is spring, additional fertilizer may be needed later in the season, when flowers are at their peak, as shown. In general, organic fertilizers can be applied plentifully, whereas inorganic materials (see next page) must be carefully measured to avoid harmful excess.

FEEDING ROSES

Organic manures: *Apply to the soil in spring. Materials include manure, bone meal, fish, hoof and horn, garden compost, wood ash, leaf mold, young green plants. It is preferable to combine animal and vegetable ingredients.*

Inorganic manures: *Apply fertilizers to the soil in spring and summer. Foliar feeds to the leaves, spring to late summer. Check all fertilizers to see if they are suitable for roses.*

A combination of organic and inorganic manures may be used.

Inorganic Manuring. The second method of feeding is known as inorganic manuring, which implies that nothing is being given to work through the living organisms of the soil. In this case a study has been made of the minerals required by plants, and they are supplied in a direct dose, ready to use as soon as they dissolve in water and encounter the roots. They may also be sprayed directly on the leaves and absorbed through them, a process called foliar feeding.

The chief elements required are nitrogen, phosphorus, and potassium, known together as NPK, under which initials their proportions are commonly indicated on a container.

Nitrogen makes plants grow fast. It forms most of the atmosphere, but is not available to plants until it is combined with other elements; this is a service naturally performed by the soil organisms, but the fertilizer industry can imitate them. The normal nitrogenous fertilizer used by rosarians is nitrate of potassium; an alternative is nitro-chalk, but not for highly alkaline soils; a good modern preparation is urea-formaldehyde (Nitroform); and the cheapest, rather too short and sudden in effect for roses, and not for use with alkaline substances, is sulfate of ammonia.

Phosphorus makes plants work well; it is like the oil which keeps the parts moving within the plant. Much of it goes into seeds, and little of it is returned in animal dung, because in animals it goes more to the bones. It is not a plain element, but exists in various combinations known as phosphates, of which rosarians favor superphosphate.

Potassium nourishes plants, by helping them form and mature their carbohydrates. It is used in the form of potash, which is a compound of potassium and oxygen. The forms normally used for roses are sulfate of potash or nitrate of potash; muriate of potash is held to be injurious.

In addition to these three major materials, roses also use traces of calcium, magnesium, boron, and iron, the latter two in very small quantities, which if exceeded are probably more injurious than a shortage.

The inorganic materials needed by roses are blended into rose fertilizers or foliar feeds by many manufacturers, and sold for feeding roses.

Fertilizers can be applied in spring, after pruning; and a frosty morning is a good time to do it, because the fertilizer is absorbed into the soil by the thaw. From that time, a monthly application can be made if first-class results are required; but in frosty countries it must cease about the time the first flush of blooms is over, or else the plants will bear too much soft wood in the winter. The exception to this rule is sulfate of potash, which aids the ripening process, and

Inorganic mixtures—of nitrogen, phosphorus. and potassium—can be bought already blended. For most people these mixtures are perfectly adequate, and only specialists or large-scale growers will wish to mix their own raw materials. Hardy shrub roses and climbers (like Rosa rugosa alba *above, and* R. helenae *at right) profit as much from feeding as do the newer hybrids.*

may with advantage be applied late in summer, at about 60 grams per square meter (2 ounces per square yard).

Foliar feeds have an immediate effect and are particularly useful at the height of the growing season, to add that extra touch of quality. Their use may continue later in the summer than that of fertilizers. They are especially useful to help plants which do not seem to be as happy as they should be. If they cannot get food from the soil, why not help them?

Inorganic fertilizers are useless without water, and if applied to dry soil, they may be largely wasted. They may either be hoed into the soil or watered in. Some people are so fond of their roses that they apply fertilizer in the rain.

Rates of use of inorganic fertilizers are usually printed on the container; and by a simple sum, one knows how much ground the packet should feed. Do not exceed the recommended rate; think of these things as medicines, of which an overdose can be harmful. If no rate of use is known, about 60 grams per square meter (2 ounces per square yard) is a fair rule; but if one is dealing with the trace elements, the quantities needed are minute.

Inorganic fertilizers contain substances, usually described as salts, which are used neither by the plants nor by the soil organisms; they are eventually disposed of by being washed away into the subsoil, out of reach of the plants. But if the supply of water is ineffective in so removing them, then they can in time adversely affect growth. The answer is to flood them away. This trouble may be suspected if plants fail to continue their momentum of growth in kind, early summer weather, after a promising start in spring; it is not normal in regions of adequate rainfall.

In order to achieve the perfect blooms illustrated here in close-up, it may be necessary to do some special remedial feeding in addition to the basic preparatory dosages. Slow-blooming plants could require extra nitrogen; weak-stemmed, sagging plants may benefit from a higher dose of phosphorus. At the height of the growing season, foliar feeding can be beneficial: chemical products mixed with water are sprayed directly on the leaves for rapid absorption.

The two fine specimens shown above are 'Kordes' Perfecta' and 'Alec's Red.'

HEALTH

It is a rule of nature that one form of life is the food for another. Humans, for example, eat chickens and wheat; and roses are food in the opinion of certain animals, insects, fungi, and viruses. The object of the rose grower is to deny those organisms their food, a project which requires some

Damaged blooms, such as this unfortunate rose hurt by bad weather, must be removed and discarded. Many other rose problems—pests in particular—can be deterred or fought.

Above right: When it comes to predatory allies, the rosarian's best friend is the ladybug (or ladybird), such as one shown here in the act of eating a greenfly aphid.

resolution, because although a greenfly is a mild-mannered creature, it is as set on eating its dinner as any tiger.

The first step toward healthy roses is to grow them well, and to plant varieties which naturally have some resistance to fungus diseases. To sell and recommend such roses ought to be the duty of every reputable nurseryman.

The second step is to recognize each enemy and deter it immediately. Deterrence consists of excluding the enemy, or encouraging organisms that devour him, or applying such substances as will either kill him, or render his proposed meal obnoxious to him. As a last resort, it may be necessary to destroy diseased or damaged plants.

Exclusion applies to animal pests. Young rose shoots or leaves are attractive to many herbivores, such as deer, cows, goats, and rabbits. The bark of rose stems attracts rabbits, hares, and mice. With the exception of the last named, these creatures must be fenced out of reach of the roses.

The predatory allies of the rose grower may well include a cat and a dog to deal with mice and rabbits; but in the main the allies are birds and insects, which reduce but do not usually exterminate the insect enemies of the rose. Nearly all small birds are to be encouraged. The most beneficial insect is the ladybird (ladybug); spiders are helpful; and although he is generally unwelcome, the wasp is also a useful predator. Rose growers in warmer countries should look with approval upon the praying mantis.

The final guardian is the rose grower. Sooner or later the ravenous hordes will certainly find their way in; and once they have gained entry, they multiply exceedingly fast. For that reason, their early apprehension is the best means of

These roses are afflicted with a disease known as rose gall (or robin's pincushion), which fortunately is not the most common rose ailment.

Above right: *Spraying to counteract blackspot (see also page 168). Great caution must be exercised with all sprays.*

Left: *A harmful insect: the cuckoospit or rose froghopper.*

controlling them. If the first signs of a particular insect or fungus are removed manually, the attack may be averted. The appropriate remedy should be applied without any delay, immediately the attack is perceived. The reason that roses suffer an epidemic is almost always because the early signs were not observed.

The remedies are generally in the form of chemical compounds toxic to the enemy, designed to be diluted and sprayed onto the plants. For these substances, whether they are stated to be safe or otherwise, strict safety precautions should be observed:

They should be stored out of reach of children.

They should be kept in their original containers; or if transferred, they should be labeled so clearly as to obviate the least chance of mistake. The maker's instructions should be studied and obeyed.

The operator should keep toxic substances off his skin and out of his respiratory system, by wearing such protective gloves or masks as may be necessary. He should not spray against the wind. And he should wash himself afterward.

To avoid scorching the foliage, spraying should not be done in strong sun; on such a day, wait for evening.

Insect Enemies. The most common is the greenfly, which is an aphid or plant louse, to be found clustered on the youngest, tenderest parts of the rose shoot, from which it sucks the sap. Birds and ladybirds eat them, fingers and thumbs, or cold rain can reduce them. Failing those remedies, there are in most countries a number of aphid (greenfly) killers on the market, simple to use and effective in results. At the present time, the most effective active ingredients are considered to be dimethoate, formothion, menazon, and malathion. The product probably bears a different name, such as Greenfly killer, with the active ingredients stated on the container in small print.

Caterpillars of various kinds can reduce rose leaves to a skeleton of veins, and often burrow into flowers. Occasional caterpillars may be handpicked, but a deterrent spray is a good safeguard; effective active ingredients are trichlorphon and fenitrothion; malathion also has some deterrent effect. Some beetles are also deterred by the treatment for caterpillars.

Thrips, or thunderflies, intrude as the bud is barely open, and multiply in warm humid weather, quite spoiling the blooms. The same active ingredients as for aphids are a deterrent, with the possible exception of menazon.

Scale insects live on the bark of roses, as a kind of crust, which may be white, brown, or peppery. They suck the sap out of the stems they inhabit. It may be possible to cut off such a stem and burn it; or else they may be sprayed, best with products which contain either dimethoate, formothion, malathion; or paraffin emulsion may be used. It can be mixed at home with equal amounts of paraffin and pure water, with a little washing-up liquid, diluted before use at 40 milliliters to the liter ($1\frac{1}{2}$ fluid ounces per quart) of water.

Leaf-hoppers are small, pale yellowish insects which live on the underside of the leaves, from which they suck sap. The result of their operations may be seen by pale mottled marks on the upper side of the leaves, and by the molted skins they discard on the undersides. They are too agile to be removed manually, but the sprays recommended for aphids will deal with them.

Red spider mite is a destructive pest. It should be suspected when pale pinprick marks are seen on the leaves. Examine the underside for creatures like red lice, so small that a magnifying glass will be helpful. They leave traces of web and move slowly. They are busy sucking the life out of the leaves. If they have arrived in strength, remove and burn the worst affected leaves, which are usually near the base of the

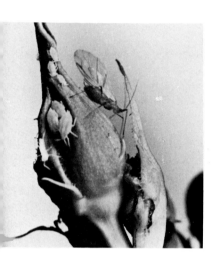

Rose aphids are the commonest of the insect enemies. Two varieties of aphid are seen attacking a bud: the winged greenfly at right, and the smaller wingless redfly. Aphids can be fought with commercial sprays.

Capsid bugs cause damaged and misshapen leaves. The bugs, larger than aphids and green or brown in color, feed on the sap of roses.

plant. Red spider likes dry conditions, so water will be some discouragement. Paraffin emulsion is recommended; this insect is not easy to control, and the killers used commercially are somewhat too dangerous for gardeners.

Some insects are transient visitors, calling to lay their eggs or collect pieces of leaf for their nests. Roses which have been sprayed with insecticides are not likely to attract them. The leaf-rolling sawfly is a case in point; it lays its eggs, and

Rose bark is susceptible to scale insects, which form a white, brown, or mixed crust and suck the sap from the stem.

Above right: Leaf-cutting bees remove round pieces of leaf to be used for their nests.

Red spider mite, a tiny insect found on the underside of rose leaves and (as in the photograph) the leaves of other plants. It causes pale pinprick marks on the leaves and is difficult to control.

injects a toxin to cause the leaf to roll up, an excellent cradle for the young sawfly, which hatches out a few days later. If this occurs, remove and burn the leaves.

Some insects are regional, rather than general; for example, white ants, against which Bordeaux mixture, or sprays containing copper sulfate should be watered on the ground, or on the base of the plant, remembering that some foliage damage is likely; or the undiluted powder may be sprinkled on the soil. There are many regional beetles, such as the Japanese beetle, with voracious appetites for rose leaves. Local advice as to specialized measures should be sought in these cases; an old Chinese trick with beetles is to put out a container of dung overnight, and next day kill the beetles attracted into it.

Our list of insect pests is of course incomplete, limited to the most frequent and likely of these enemies. Many others may be encountered, such as the leaf-cutting bees and the capsid bugs, both of whose handiwork is illustrated on these pages. At nighttime, your roses may play host to the dark-brown earwig which will nibble away at petals and and leaves. His daytime retreat (nearby woods or dead leaves) can be sprayed.

Rolled leaves, which have been injected with a toxin by the leaf-curling sawfly that lays its eggs here. Such leaves must be removed and burned.

Fungus Enemies. The three main types are mildew, blackspot, and rust. Since natural predators will not destroy them, the rose grower must take appropriate action.

Mildew, a gray mold, is very common. Unless the site is to blame, mildew is easily kept under control by sprays with such active ingredients as benomyl, triforine, bupirimate-triforine, thiophanate-methyl, triadimefon, and fenarimol.

Blackspot must be treated promptly or else the roses will be

The insect known as the slug saw-fly can cause severe leaf damage.

Above right: Rose rust grows on the underside of leaves, usually beginning low on the plant. Early evidence is small yellow pinprick marks on the upper surface; underneath, one will see clusters of orange or black pustules.

Right: Mildew is a gray mold, usually first seen on young shoots or around the ovary beneath the flower bud. Incipient mildew often shows up as bumps on young leaves. It can be encouraged by halted growth, a poor site, cold weather, or drought.
Mildew is seen here on shoots and beneath rose buds.

almost leafless by the end of the season. The most effective active ingredients are benomyl, triforine, bupirimate-triforine, thiophanate-methyl, and fenarimol. Badly affected leaves may be collected and burned; and the same goes for fallen leaves in winter. A winter spray of Bordeaux mixture will help kill overwintering spores.

Rose rust, which grows on the underside of the leaves, can be controlled by the active ingredient oxycarboxin; others are benodanil, maneb, zineb, thiram, and mancozeb. The recommendations about leaves and a winter spray are the same as under blackspot.

Virus Enemies. Viruses inhabit nearly all living organisms, but do not necessarily cause the destruction of their hosts. In roses, they may be assumed to be latent, and to be passed from one plant to another most commonly by biting or sucking insects, but also by the gardener's tools.

The worst virus is rose wilt, which may cause a shoot, or even the whole plant, to collapse and die. This usually happens when the plant is in full growth, and seems to its owner quite inexplicable. One must remove and burn the plant. Rose mosaic does not appear to hinder the plant. It may be seen as intricate and symmetrical yellow patterns traced on the leaves.

Blackspot, as the name suggests, is seen as irregular black circles upon the leaves. It spreads very fast, usually appearing low on the plant at first.

PRUNING

Pruning is very simple, once one reduces it to a clear concept. It is merely the removal of such parts of the plant as are unsuitable to bear good flowers. Once one learns how to recognize those parts, there is no problem at all.

Where and how to make the cut is elementary common sense: just above a growth point (otherwise known as an eye) and on a slant to match the line of dying back to the growth point. The degree of slant can be learned by looking at some roses which were pruned last year. If a mistake is made, it does not greatly matter, because the stub can be trimmed off in a few weeks when the growth point has made itself more evident.

When to prune is also common sense: do it when the plants are dormant, because then they bleed less, and have fewer leaves to interrupt a clear view of the stems. If climbers are pruned at the autumn side of dormancy, they can also be tied safely for winter; bushes might as well be allowed to wait until early spring, for they look less attractive after being pruned. If the climate allows no dormant period, pruning is done piecemeal between flowering times.

In fact, every time a flower is cut, or deadheaded, or when the plants are trimmed to guard against winter winds, then some kind of summer or autumn pruning has been done.

Tools are important, because bad ones can injure the wood. Efficient secateurs should be used; stems too large for secateurs should be cut by a thin-bladed pruning saw.

The wood to be judged unsuitable for bearing good flowers falls into these categories: too old, damaged, too thin, too crowded.

Old wood is recognized by the state of its bark, which has passed through the stages of being green and smooth, and has become dark, dry, and probably wrinkled. It is not judged on its appearance, but on what it is bearing. If it is the supporter of strong, young shoots, then it is kept. If among its superstructure there is nothing better than thin twigs, then it is cut out to the base. There is a third possibility, that a side branch may carry strong wood, but the old shoot may be barren above that side branch; if so, it should be cut off immediately above that juncture.

Damaged wood is recognized in two ways: by an inspection of the bark for wounds, which are often caused by tools; and by an inspection of the pith to see if it is frozen or immature. If a prominent wound is found on the bark, cut below it. Such wounds often get canker and are best away.

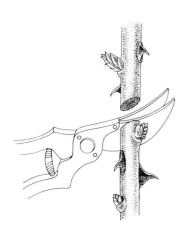

The technique: Pruning is done just above a growth point (or eye), on a slant running back to the level of the growth point. The exact degree of slant is best learned by observing other pruned plants. Good clippers or secateurs are needed: for very thick stems one must use a pruning saw.

PRUNING

Definition

Pruning is the removal of branches (or parts of them) that will not bear good flowers.

Which branches should be pruned: *Those which are*

— *too old*
— *damaged*
— *too thin*
— *too crowded*

When to prune: *During dormant seasons (late autumn to early spring). If the climate allows no dormant period, pruning is done piecemeal between flowering times.*

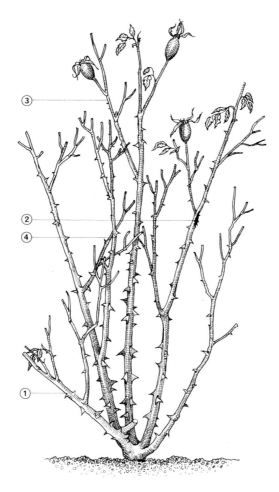

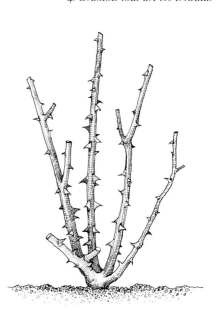

Climbers are one of the three types of rose that require special pruning. The main task with climbers is to shorten the side shoots to encourage flowers, rather than an overhang, the year after.

To inspect the pith, make a trial cut across the stem high up. A sound shoot has firm white wood, with a narrow ring of pith at is center. Frozen shoots have discolored pith, gray to brown in color. Frozen stems should be shortened until white pith is reached. Every rose grower in frosty countries knows that this process very often ends at the base of the plant; and it is in fact the main reason for severe pruning. Immature pith is treated the same way. It is usually gray and crumbly, instead of firm and white, and was not sufficiently ripe before dormancy began.

Having removed old wood and damaged wood, the rose grower should now be looking at a plant composed purely of wood that is willing to grow. Much of it will be too thin to carry a good flower. The desirable thickness varies from variety to variety, and until those variations are learned from handling flowers in summer, the rose grower can employ a simple general method by asking himself the following.

Suppose he was cutting flowers in the summer, what thickness of stem would he expect to put in a vase? Imagine the answer, and shorten all the thin shoots to a point of the imagined thickness of the summer cut. Some of the thin

A rose plant before and after pruning. The numerals refer to the four types of wood (listed above) that must be pruned. The rules are essentially simple. Three types of rose (shown in the three photographs on these pages) offer exceptions to the basic rules.

shoots will disappear altogether on that supposition. The grower should carefully observe next summer how right or wrong he was for each variety, according to the flower stems it has borne in response to his work.

That is the way to learn to prune, by observing results.

The final category of shoots is those which are too crowded. Here the beginner should be cautious, for he is likely to throw away good wood for no good purpose. Nature can accommodate her crowded shoots better than we normally suppose. Be content with removing, or shortening, the smaller of two shoots which actually rub together.

One can always cut again later on. One cannot put a cut shoot back.

Properly interpreted, these rules cover the pruning of all roses. But it is helpful to spell them out for special cases:

Climbers and trailers often make a long shoot, with few or no flowers on it, and bloom in future years on side shoots from it. Therefore, in their case, the main pruning is normally to shorten the side shoots to a point where they are thick enough to bear another flowering stem. If the mistake is made of leaving them too long, they will in two or three years develop an overhang.

In Standard (or Tree) roses, the base is to be taken as the union between the head and the stem; it is not the ground level. Their powers of regeneration are less than those of bushes, and the pruning should, in cases of doubt, be less severe.

Many Rugosas have young basal shoots which look promising, but prove to flop over when in leaf. They need to be pruned a little more severely than one thought. But these, and many roses grown as specimen shrubs, may be trimmed lightly, and only pruned in a thorough way once every four or five years.

Roses which are not remontant, including many of the old-fashioned types, are likely to bear a number of long, thin shoots, which did not flower last season but are intended to bear blooms next summer. They must not be cut short or else the flowers would be lost. Cut the thin ends off, and leave on the plant about two-thirds of the shoots.

Many wild roses need special treatment (see picture, right). Young bush roses, newly planted, should be pruned severely; for no matter whether their wood is sound, their roots are being obliged to make a new start, and they do not require more than two or three eyes per stem to support during the first few months.

If any plant is known to have virus, or suspicious symptoms, prune it last, and then disinfect the tools.

Rugosas are another special case, as far as pruning is concerned. Particular attention should be paid to their young basal shoots, which often prove too weak.

Many wild roses have single flowers of inconsiderable weight. Their thin shoots therefore can quite well sustain the blooms. In particular, their long, arching shoots should be left at full length, for they are one of the graces of the plants. As there are so few pieces to prune out, these wild roses may generally be left until some old portions are noticed as being due for removal.

Overleaf (page 172): 'Veilchenblau,' a violet-colored rambler.

APPENDIX:
VITAL STATISTICS ON 300 ADDITIONAL ROSE VARIETIES

Name	Year introduced	Class (See abbreviations list below)	Color (Shaded)	Form (All double except single & semi-double)	Flower size	Freedom of flower (R = Remontant)	Scent (1–10)	Growth	Habit	Best use
Adolf Horstmann	1971	HT	Yellow (red)	Pointed	Very large	R moderate	3	Bush	Normal	Cutting
Aimée Vibert	1828	Nois	White	Full	Medium	R moderate	4	Climber	Upright	Pillar
Akebono	1964	HT	Lt yellow	Pointed	Very large	R moerate	3	Bush	Normal	Show
Albertine	1921	Wich H	Pink	Full	Medium	Summer	4	Climber	Vigorous	Pergola
Alison Wheatcroft	1959	Flor	Orange red	Thin	Medium	R average	3	Bush	Restrained	Bedding
Aloha	1949	Cl HT	Pink	Full	Medium	R average	3	Climber	Short	Wall, pillar
Alpha (Meinastur)	1979	HT	Scarlet	Pointed	Medium	R good	2	Bush	Normal	Cutting (glass)
Alpine Sunset	1974	HT	Lt peach	Pointed	Very large	R average	5	Bush	Short	Bedding
Amatsu Otome	1960	HT	Yellow	Pointed	Very large	R average	4	Bush	Normal	Cutting
American Pillar	1902	Setig H	Carmine (white)	Single	Small	Summer	1	Climber	Vigorous	Pergola
Amy Robsart	1894	Eglan H	Pink	Semi-dble	Medium	Summer	6	Bush	Tall, wide	Shrub
Andrewsii	c 1820	Spin H	Pink (cream)	Semi-dble	Small	Late spring	4	Bush	Very short	Border
Angel Face	1968	Flor	Lilac	Open	Medium	R good	4	Bush	Normal	Border
Anna Wheatcroft	1958	Flor	Vermilion	Semi-dble	Medium	R good	3	Bush	Normal	Bedding
Anne of Geierstein	1894	Eglan H	Crimson	Single	Small	Summer	6	Bush	Tall, wide	Shrub
Apricot Nectar	1965	Flor	Pale apricot	Semi-dble	Large	R good	5	Bush	Normal	Cutting, bedding
Baby Gold Star	1940	Min	Yellow	Full	Very small	R moderate	2	Bush	Small	Border, pot
Baccara	1956	HT	Scarlet	Pointed	Medium	R good	2	Bush	Upright	Cutting (glass)
Baronne Edmond de Rothschild	1969	HT	Red/silvery	Pointed	Large	R good	5	Bush	Normal	Bedding
Beauty Secret	1965	Min	Red	Open	Very small	R good	2	Bush	Small	Border, pot
Belinda	1936	Poly	Pink	Single	Very small	R average	2	Bush	Tall	Shrub
Belinda (Tanbeedee)	1971	Flor	Orange	Neat	Medium	R good	4	Bush	Normal	Cutting (glass)
Belle Amour	c 1850	Alba	Lt pink	Semi-dble	Medium	Summer	5	Bush	Tall	Shrub
Belle de Crécy	c 1848	Gallica	Mauve	Full	Large	Summer	7	Bush	Lax	Shrub
Benson & Hedges Gold (Macgem)	1979	HT	Yellow	Pointed	Large	R good	5	Bush	Normal	Bedding
Betty Prior	1935	Flor	Pink	Single	Small	R excellent	3	Bush	Normal	Bedding
Blanc Double de Coubert	1892	Rug H	White	Open	Medium	R average	5	Bush	Rounded	Shrub
Blanche Moreau	1880	Moss	White	Open	Medium	Summer	3	Bush	Upright	Shrub
Blaze	1932	Cl Poly	Scarlet	Semi-dble	Small	Summer	2	Climber	Vigorous	Pillar
Bloomfield Abundance	1920	H China	Lt pink	Neat	Small	R good	2	Bush	Wide	Shrub
Bobby Charlton	1974	HT	Pink	Pointed	Very large	R moderate	3	Bush	Upright	Show, cutting
Bonfire Night	1971	Flor	Orange red	Semi-dble	Small	R good	3	Bush	Normal	Bedding
Boule de Neige	1867	Bourb	White	Full	Large	R moderate	8	Bush	Upright	Shrub, pillar
Bourbon Queen	1834	Bourb	Pink	Open	Small	R average	3	Bush	Wide	Shrub
Buccaneer	1952	HT	Yellow	Thin	Medium	R good	4	Bush	Tall	Shrub, pillar
Bullata	c 1800	Cent	Pink	Low center	Medium	Summer	5	Bush	Tall	Shrub
Busy Lizzie	1970	Flor	Pink	Semi-dble	Medium	R very good	4	Bush	Normal	Bedding
Camaieux	1830	Gallica	Purple/white	Quartered	Small	Summer	3	Bush	Lax	Shrub
Cardinal de Richelieu	1840	Gallica	Purple	Full	Small	Summer	4	Bush	Restrained	Shrub
Carol Amling	1953	Flor	Pink	Neat	Medium	R good	2	Bush	Normal	Cutting (glass)
Casino	1963	Cl HT	Yellow	Pointed	Large	R good	4	Climber	Restrained	Warm wall
Cécile Brunner Climbing	1894	H China	Lt pink	Neat	Small	Summer	2	Climber	Vigorous	Fence, wall
Celsiana	c 1750	Damask	Pink	Semi-dble	Medium	Summer	4	Bush	Tall	Shrub
Charles de Mills	c 1840	Gallica	Crimson	Full	Medium	Summer	4	Bush	Restrained	Shrub
Chinatown	1963	Flor	Yellow	Open	Medium	R good	5	Bush	Tall, wide	Shrub, hedge
Chorus (Meijulita)	1975	Flor	Crimson	Open	Large	R good	3	Bush	Normal	Bedding
Chrysler Imperial	1952	HT	Crimson	Pointed	Large	R average	8	Bush	Normal	Cutting
Circus Parade	1963	Flor	Orange red	Open	Medium	R good	3	Bush	Normal	Bedding
City of Belfast	1968	Flor	Scarlet	Full	Small	R very good	3	Bush	Short	Bedding
City of Leeds	1966	Flor	Pink	Open	Medium	R excellent	3	Bush	Normal	Bedding

Name	Year introduced	Class (See abbreviations list below)	Color (Shaded)	Form (All double except single & semi-double)	Flower size	Freedom of flower (R = Remontant)	Scent (1–10)	Growth	Habit	Best use
Cocktail	1957	Cl Flor	Red (yellow)	Single	Small	R good	4	Bush	Tall, lax	Shrub, pillar
Common Moss	c 1720	Moss	Pink	Neat	Medium	Summer	4	Bush	Tall, lax	Fence, shrub
Coventry Cathedral	1972	Flor	Lt vermilion	Open	Medium	R good	3	Bush	Normal	Bedding
Crimson Shower	1951	Wich H	Crimson	Pompon	Very small	Summer (late)	2	Trailer	Tenuous	Pillar, fence
Dainty Bess	1925	HT	Lt Pink	Single	Large	R good	3	Bush	Normal	Cutting, shrub
Dainty Maid	1938	Flor	Pink	Single	Medium	R very good	3	Bush	Normal	Hedge, bedding
Darling Flame (Minuetto)	1971	Min	Orange red	Neat	Very small	R good	2	Bush	Small	Border, pot
Dearest	1960	Flor	Pink	Open	Medium	R very good	5	Bush	Normal	Bedding
De Meaux	c 1789	Cent	Pink	Pompon	Small	Summer	6	Bush	Compact	Shrub
Diamond Jubilee	1947	HT	Buff	Pointed	Very large	R good	5	Bush	Normal	Show
Doncasterii	c 1930	Macro H	Rose red	Single	Medium	Summer	4	Bush	Wide	Shrub (hips)
Dorothy Perkins	1901	Wich H	Pink	Pompon	Small	Summer	2	Climber	Vigorous	Fence, pergola
Double Delight	1976	HT	White/red	Pointed	Very large	R good	7	Bush	Upright	Cutting
Dr. W. van Fleet	1910	Wich H	Blush	Open	Medium	Summer	5	Climber	Vigorous	Pergola, wall
Duet	1960	HT	Red/pink	Pointed	Large	R good	4	Bush	Upright	Bedding, shrub
Duke of Windsor	1969	HT	Vermilion	Pointed	Large	R good	6	Bush	Normal	Bedding
Dutch Gold	1978	HT	Yellow	Pointed	Large	R good	4	Bush	Normal	Bedding
Easter Morning	1960	Min	White	Neat	Very small	R good	2	Bush	Small	Border, pot
Eden Rose	1950	HT	Pink	Pointed	Very large	R good	5	Bush	Upright	Shrub, cutting
Eiffel Tower	1963	HT	Pink	Pointed	Very large	R average	5	Bush	Normal	Show
Eleanor	1960	Min	Coral pink	Open	Very small	R average	2	Bush	Small	Border, pot
Elegance	1937	Cl HT	Lt yellow	Pointed	Large	Summer	2	Climber	Vigorous	Fence, wild area
Elizabeth of Glamis (Irish Beauty)	1964	Flor	Salmon	Pointed	Medium	R good	5	Bush	Restrained	Cutting, bedding
Emily Gray	1918	Wich H	Yellow	Thin	Medium	Summer	3	Climber	Normal	Fence
Ernest H. Morse	1965	HT	Crimson	Pointed	Large	R good	4	Bush	Normal	Bedding
Eroica	1968	HT	Crimson	Pointed	Large	R average	6	Bush	Normal	Cutting
Esther of Arim	1970	Flor	Orange red	Pointed	Medium	R average	3	Bush	Short	Cutting
Etoile de Hollande Climbing	1931	Cl HT	Crimson	Open	Large	R good	7	Climber	Vigorous	Wall
Evelyn Fison (Irish Wonder)	1962	Flor	Bright red	Open	Medium	R excellent	3	Bush	Normal	Bedding
Evening Star	1974	HT	White	Pointed	Large	R very good	4	Bush	Normal	Bedding, cutting
Eye Paint	1976	Flor	Red/white	Single	Small	R very good	2	Bush	Wide	Shrub
Fairy Moss	1969	Min	Rose red	Semi-dble	Very small	R moderate	2	Bush	Small	Border, pot
Fashion	1949	Flor	Coral pink	Open	Medium	R good	3	Bush	Restrained	Cutting
Félicité Parmentier	c 1800	Alba	Blush	Quartered	Medium	Summer	3	Bush	Wide	Shrub
First Prize	1970	HT	Rose red	Pointed	Very large	R average	5	Bush	Upright	Show
Fountain	1970	Flor	Crimson	Open	Large	R excellent	4	Bush	Tall	Shrub
Fragrant Delight	1978	Flor	Orange pink	Semi-dble	Large	R very good	6	Bush	Normal	Bedding
François Juranville	1906	Wich H	Pink	Open	Small	Summer	4	Climber	Vigorous	Pergola, fence
Frau Karl Druschki	1901	H Perp	White	Pointed	Very large	R good	1	Bush	Tall	Shrub
Fred Loads	1967	Flor	Vermilion	Semi-dble	Large	R very good	3	Bush	Upright	Shrub
Fred Streeter	1951	Moy H	Pink	Single	Medium	Summer	2	Bush	Tall, wide	Shrub (hips)
Freude (Dekorat)	1974	HT	Coral pink	Pointed	Large	R good	4	Bush	Normal	Bedding, cutting
Frühlingsmorgen	1942	Spin H	Pink	Single	Large	Summer	5	Bush	Wide	Shrub
Garden Party	1959	HT	Cream (pink)	Pointed	Large	R good	3	Bush	Normal	Bedding
Garnette	1947	Flor	Red	Neat	Medium	R good	2	Bush	Normal	Cutting (glass)
Général Schablikine	1879	Tea	Copper red	Quartered	Medium	R good	3	Bush	Tall	Shrub
Glenfiddich	1976	Flor	Amber	Neat	Medium	R good	4	Bush	Normal	Bedding
Gloire de Dijon	1853	Nois	Buff	Full	Large	R moderate	4	Climber	Normal	Wall
Gloire des Rosomanes (Ragged Robin)	1825	Bourb	Red	Semi-dble	Large	R average	4	Bush	Tall	Pillar
Golden Scepter (Spek's Yellow)	1947	HT	Dp yellow	Pointed	Medium	R good	3	Bush	Leggy	Cutting
Golden Slippers	1961	Flor	Orange pink	Semi-dble	Medium	R good	4	Bush	Short	Border
Goldfinch	1907	Cl Poly	Yellow to white	Semi-dble	Small	Summer	6	Climber	Normal	Pillar
Grand Hotel	1972	Cl HT	Scarlet	Full	Large	R good	3	Climber	Restrained	Wall
Greensleeves	1980	Flor	Blush to green	Semi-dble	Large	R average	1	Bush	Upright	Curiosity
Gruss an Teplitz	1897	H China	Crimson	Open	Small	R good	4	Bush	Tall	Shrub
Guinée	1938	Cl HT	Dark red	Pointed	Medium +	Summer	4	Climber	Normal	Fence
Hamburger Phoenix	1957	Kord H	Red	Semi-dble	Medium	R moderate	1	Climber	Normal	Pillar
Harry Wheatcroft	1973	HT	Striped	Pointed	Large	R good	2	Bush	Compact	Cutting
Heidelberg	1959	Flor	Crimson	Full	Medium +	R good	1	Bush	Tall	Shrub
Honey Favorite	1962	HT	Buff pink	Pointed	Very large	R good	2	Bush	Normal	Show
Honeymoon (Honigmond)	1960	Flor	Yellow	Open	Medium	R good	4	Bush	Normal	Bedding
Hugh Dickson	1905	H Perp	Crimson	Open	Large	R average	5	Bush	Tall, lax	Shrub

Name	Year introduced	Class (See abbreviations list below)	Color (Shaded)	Form (All double except single & semi-double)	Flower size	Freedom of flower (R = Remontant)	Scent (1–10)	Growth	Habit	Best use
Iced Ginger	1971	Flor	Blush (orange)	Pointed	Large	R good	4	Bush	Upright	Bedding, cutting
Ice White	1966	Flor	White	Open	Medium +	R good	3	Bush	Upright	Bedding
Irish Mist	1967	Flor	Orange red	Open	Medium	R very good	4	Bush	Normal	Bedding
Isabel de Ortiz	1962	HT	Deep pink	Pointed	Very large	R average	4	Bush	Normal	Show
Janet's Pride	1892	Eglan H	Pink (white)	Open	Medium	Summer	5	Bush	Tall	Shrub
Joseph's Coat	1964	Flor	Yellow/red	Thin	Medium	R good	3	Bush	Vigorous	Shrub
Joyce Northfield	1978	HT	Lt yellow	Pointed	Large	R good	4	Bush	Normal	Cutting
Judy Fischer	1968	Min	Pink	Neat	Very small	R average	2	Bush	Small	Border, pot
Judy Garland	1977	Flor	Yellow (red)	Full	Large	R good	5	Bush	Normal	Bedding
Kara	1970	Min	Pink	Single	Very small	R moderate	2	Bush	Small	Border, pot
Kathleen Harrop	1919	Bourbon	Lt pink	Quartered	Medium	R moderate	5	Climber	Normal	Pillar
Kiftsgate	1954	Filip H	White	Single	Small	Summer	6	Trailer	Very vigorous	Through tree
Kim	1973	Flor	Yellow (red)	Full	Medium	R good	3	Bush	Short	Bedding
King's Ransom	1961	HT	Yellow	Pointed	Large	R average	3	Bush	Normal	Cutting
Königin der Rosen (Color Wonder)	1964	HT	Orange red (cream)	Pointed	Large	R average	3	Bush	Normal	Cutting
Königin von Dänemark	1826	Alba	Pink	Incurved	Medium	Summer	8	Bush	Tall	Shrub
Kronenburg	1965	HT	Purple/yellow	Pointed	Very large	R good	3	Bush	Vigorous	Shrub
Lady Hillingdon Climbing	1917	Cl Tea	Apricot yellow	Pointed	Large	R average	5	Climber	Normal	Wall
Lady Sylvia	1926	HT	Pink	Pointed	Large	R very good	7	Bush	Normal	Cutting
La France	1867	HT	Pink	Pointed	Large	R average	2	Bush	Normal	Historic
Laneii	1846	Moss	Purple	Full	Large	Summer	4	Bush	Wide	Shrub
Lavender Lassie	1959	Flor	Lilac	Full	Medium	R good	6	Bush	Vigorous	Shrub
Lawrence Johnston	1923	Foet H	Yellow	Semi-dble	Medium	Summer	6	Climber	Normal	Wall
Letchworth Garden City (Harkover)	1978	Flor	Pink	Thin	Medium	R very good	3	Bush	Normal	Bedding
Little Buckaroo	1956	Min	Red	Thin	Small	R good	3	Bush	Short	Border
Little Darling	1956	Flor	Yellow/pink	Open	Medium	R good	4	Bush	Normal	Bedding
Little Flirt	1961	Min	Yellow/pink	Open	Medium	R good	2	Bush	Short	Border
Little White Pet	1879	Semp H	White	Pompon	Small	R good	3	Bush	Short	Border
Liverpool Echo	1971	Flor	Salmon	Full	Medium	R very good	2	Bush	Normal	Bedding
Louise Odier	1851	Bourb	Pink	Open	Medium	R average	5	Bush	Upright	Shrub
Magenta	1954	Flor	Purple	Full	Medium	R average	7	Bush	Tall, lax	Shrub
Maiden's Blush	c 1790	Alba	Blush	Incurved	Medium	Summer	5	Bush	Tall	Shrub
Manning's Blush	c 1832	Eglan H	Blush	Full	Small	Summer	4	Bush	Compact	Shrub
Marie Pavié	1888	Poly	Pink	Open	Medium	R good	4	Bush	Short	Border
Marjorie Fair	1977	Poly	Red/white	Single	Very small	R good	1	Bush	Wide	Shrub
Mary Summer	1975	Flor	Orange pink	Open	Medium	R good	3	Bush	Vigorous	Bedding
Masquerade	1949	Flor	Yellow/red	Semi-dble	Medium	R good	3	Bush	Normal	Bedding
Matangi	1974	Flor	Red/white	Open	Medium	R very good	2	Bush	Normal	Bedding
Max Graf	1919	Wich H	Pink	Single	Medium	Summer	2	Trailer	Vigorous	Ground cover
Maxima	c 1750	Alba	White	Rounded	Medium	Summer	5	Bush	Tall, wide	Shrub
Meg	1954	Cl Flor	Apricot pink	Semi-dble	Large	R moderate	4	Climber	Normal	Fence
Memoriam	1961	HT	Blush	Pointed	Very large	R moderate	6	Bush	Restrained	Show
Mercedes	1974	Flor	Vermilion	Pointed	Medium	R very good	2	Bush	Normal	Cutting (glass)
Meteor	1959	Flor	Scarlet	Open	Medium	R good	1	Bush	Short	Border
Mister Lincoln	1964	HT	Crimson	Pointed	Large	R moderate	7	Bush	Normal	Cutting
Mme Alfred Carrière	1879	Nois	White	Full	Large	R average	5	Climber	Normal	Wall
Mme Butterfly	1918	HT	Blush	Pointed	Large	R very good	7	Bush	Normal	Cutting
Mme Ernst Calvat	1888	Bourb	Pink	Full	Large	R moderate	6	Bush	Vigorous, lax	Shrub
Mme Isaac Pereire	1881	Bourb	Purple pink	Full	Large	R moderate	6	Bush	Vigorous, lax	Shrub
Mme Legras de St. Germain	c 1840	Alba	White	Round	Large	Summer	6	Bush	Tall	Shrub
Mme Louis Laperrière	1952	HT	Crimson	Pointed	Medium	R good	6	Bush	Normal	Bedding
Molly McGredy	1969	Flor	Carmine/white	Pointed	Medium	R very good	2	Bush	Normal	Bedding
Montezuma	1955	HT	Carmine red	Pointed	Large	R very good	1	Bush	Vigorous	Shrub
Moonlight	1913	H Musk	Cream	Semi-dble	Medium	R good	4	Bush	Vigorous	Pillar
Morning Jewel	1968	Cl Flor	Pink	Open	Medium	R moderate	2	Climber	Restrained	Wall
Mr. Bluebird	1960	Min	Purple	Semi-dble	Very small	R average	3	Bush	Small	Border, pot
Mrs. Anthony Waterer	1898	Rug H	Crimson	Semi-dble	Medium	R moderate	5	Bush	Wide	Shrub
Mrs. Colville	c 1820	Spin H	Purple	Single	Very small	Late spring	3	Bush	Compact	Border
Mrs. John Laing	1887	H Perp	Pink	Pointed	Very large	R moderate	7	Bush	Wide	Shrub
Mrs. Sam McGredy Climbing	1937	Cl HT	Salmon	Pointed	Large	R moderate	2	Climber	Normal	Wall
Mullard Jubilee (Electron)	1970	HT	Pink	Pointed	Very large	R good	5	Bush	Normal	Bedding
Nathalie Nypels	1919	Flor	Pink	Semi-dble	Medium	R very good	2	Bush	Short	Border
News	1968	Flor	Purple	Thin	Medium	R very good	3	Bush	Normal	Border

Name	Year introduced	Class (See abbreviations list below)	Color (Shaded)	Form (All double except single & semi-double)	Flower size	Freedom of flower (R = Remontant)	Scent (1–10)	Growth	Habit	Best use
Nozomi	1968	Cl Min	White	Single	Very small	Summer	1	Trailer	Restrained	Ground cover
Nuits de Young	1845	Moss	Purple red	Open	Small	Summer	2	Bush	Lax	Shrub
Ocaru (Angela Rippon)	1978	Poly	Salmon pink	Neat	Small	R good	2	Bush	Short	Border, pot
Old Blush	1752	H China	Pink	Open	Medium	R very good	3	Bush	Open	Border
Old Master	1974	Flor	Red/white	Open	Large	R good	3	Bush	Vigorous	Shrub
Orangeade	1959	Flor	Vermilion	Semi-dble	Medium	R good	3	Bush	Normal	Bedding
Orange Sensation	1961	Flor	Vermilion	Neat	Medium	R good	4	Bush	Normal	Bedding
Orange Triumph	1937	Poly	Salmon red	Semi-dble	Small	R good	2	Bush	Wide	Shrub
Paddy McGredy	1962	Flor	Carmine	Pointed	Large	R very good	3	Bush	Normal	Bedding
Papa Meilland	1963	HT	Crimson	Pointed	Very large	R average	9	Bush	Shy	Cutting
Paprika	1958	Flor	Bright red	Semi-dble	Medium	R excellent	3	Bush	Normal	Bedding
Parkdirektor Riggers	1957	Kord H	Crimson	Semi-dble	Medium	R moderate	2	Climber	Normal	Pillar
Paul's Lemon Pillar	1915	Cl HT	Cream	Pointed	Very large	Summer	3	Climber	Normal	Wall
Paul's Scarlet Climber	1916	Cl Poly	Scarlet	Semi-dble	Medium	Summer	2	Climber	Normal	Fence
Peer Gynt	1968	HT	Yellow (red)	Pointed	Large	R good	4	Bush	Normal	Bedding
Perla de Alcanada	1944	Min	Rose red	Pompon	Very small	R good	1	Bush	Very short	Border
Perla de Montserrat	1945	Min	Pink	Neat	Very small	R average	2	Bush	Small	Border, pot
Perle d'Or	1884	H China	Blush (yellow)	Neat	Very small	R good	2	Bush	Short	Shrub
Pernille Poulsen	1965	Flor	Pink	Open	Medium	R excellent	4	Bush	Normal	Bedding
Petite de Hollande	c 1770	Cent	Pink	Pompon	Medium	Summer	3	Bush	Wide	Shrub
Pharaoh (Pharaon)	1967	HT	Scarlet	Open	Very large	R good	2	Bush	Normal	Shrub
Phyllis Bide	1923	Cl Poly	Yellow/pink	Open	Small	R excellent	2	Climber	Normal	Pillar
Picasso	1971	Flor	Red/white	Open	Medium	R average	2	Bush	Short	Shrub
Pineapple Poll	1970	Flor	Yellow/red	Neat	Medium	R average	5	Bush	Short	Cutting
Pink Elizabeth Arden (Geisha)	1964	Flor	Pink	Pointed	Large	R good	3	Bush	Normal	Bedding
Pink Grootendorst	1923	Rug H	Pink	Frilled	Small	R moderate	2	Bush	Tall	Shrub
Pink Peace	1959	HT	Pink	Open	Very large	R good	4	Bush	Normal	Shrub
Pompon Blanc Parfait	1876	Alba	White	Pompon	Medium	Summer	2	Bush	Open	Shrub
Poppy Flash (Rusticana)	1972	Flor	Vermilion	Thin	Medium	R excellent	2	Bush	Normal	Bedding
Pour Toi (Para Ti)	1946	Min	Cream	Neat	Very small	R good	2	Bush	Small	Border, pot
Président de Sèze	c 1830	Gallica	Mauve	Quartered	Medium	Summer	4	Bush	Wide	Shrub
President Herbert Hoover	1930	HT	Pink/yellow	Pointed	Large	R good	7	Bush	Tall	Shrub
Prima Ballerina	1957	HT	Pink	Pointed	Large	R good	9	Bush	Normal	Bedding
Princess Michiko	1966	Flor	Orange red	Open	Medium	R good	3	Bush	Normal	Bedding
Priscilla Burton	1978	Flor	Red/blush	Open	Large	R very good	2	Bush	Normal	Shrub
Pristine	1978	HT	Blush	Pointed	Large	R average	4	Bush	Normal	Cutting
Prosperity	1919	H Musk	Ivory	Full	Small	R good	3	Bush	Wide	Shrub
Rose des Quatre Saisons (Autumn Damask)	?	Damask	Pink	Full	Medium	R moderate	5	Bush	Open	Shrub
Ramona	1913	Laev H	Red	Single	Large	Late spring	3	Climber	Normal	Warm wall
Redgold	1967	Flor	Yellow/red	Full	Medium	R very good	4	Bush	Normal	Bedding
Red Lion	1966	HT	Carmine	Pointed	Very large	R average	4	Bush	Normal	Show
Red Planet	1970	HT	Crimson	Pointed	Large	R good	3	Bush	Normal	Bedding
Regensberg (Macyou)	1980	Flor	Blush/pink	Open	Large	R very good	4	Bush	Short	Bedding
Reine des Violettes	1860	H Perp	Purple	Full	Medium	R average	6	Bush	Tall	Shrub
Reine Victoria	1872	Bourb	Pink	Open	Large	R average	7	Bush	Upright	Shrub
Ritter von Barmstede	1959	Kord H	Pink	Open	Medium	R good	3	Climber	Normal	Pillar
Robin Hood	1927	Poly	Red/white	Semi-dble	Small	R good	2	Bush	Wide	Shrub
Roger Lambelin	1890	H Perp	Red/white	Full	Medium	R moderate	6	Bush	Upright	Shrub
Rosa Banksiae Alba-Plena	1807	Banks	White	Neat	Small	Late spring	3	Climber	Vigorous	Wall, tree
R. Caudata	c 1896	Cinn	Red	Single	Medium	Summer	4	Bush	Very large	Shrub (hips)
R. Chinensis Mutabilis (Tipo Ideale)	c 1805	Indicae	Cream to red	Single	Large	R very good	3	Bush	Wide	Shrub
R. Chinensis Viridiflora	c 1850	Indicae	Green	Full	Small	R good	1	Bush	Short	Curiosity
R. Helenae	1907	Synstyl	White	Single	Small	Summer	6	Trailer	Vigorous	Climb tree
R. Hugonis	1899	Pimp	Yellow	Single	Small	Late spring	4	Bush	Wide	Shrub
R. Macrophylla	1818	Cinn	Pink	Single	Medium	Summer	5	Bush	Very large	Shrub
R. Multibracteata	1910	Cinn	Pink	Single	Small	Summer	3	Bush	Upright	Shrub
R. Nitida	1807	Carol	Pink	Single	Small	Summer	4	Bush	Compact	Border
R. Primula	1910	Pimp	Lt yellow	Single	Medium	Late spring	6	Bush	Wide	Shrub
R. Roxburghii Normalis	1908	Platyrh	Pink	Single	Large	Summer	2	Bush	Wide	Shrub
R. Spinosissima Altaica	1820	Pimp	White	Single	Medium	Summer	5	Bush	Tall	Shrub
R. Stellata Mirifica	1916	Hesper	Pink	Single	Small	Summer	4	Bush	Restrained	Interest
R. Sweginzowii	1909	Cinn	Pink	Single	Medium	Summer	4	Bush	Tall, wide	Shrub (hips)

Name	Year introduced	Class (See abbreviations list below)	Color (Shaded)	Form (All double except single & semi-double)	Flower size	Freedom of flower (R = Remontant)	Scent (1–10)	Growth	Habit	Best use
R. Webbiana	1879	Cinn	Pink	Single	Small	Summer	4	Bush	Upright	Shrub
R. Willmottiae	1904	Cinn	Pink	Single	Small	Summer	4	Bush	Tall	Shrub
R. Woodsii Fendleri	1888	Cinn	Pink	Single	Medium	Late spring	3	Bush	Wide	Shrub
R. X Cantabrigiensis	1931	Hug H	Cream	Single	Medium	Late spring	4	Bush	Large	Shrub
R. X Dupontii	c 1817	Mosch H	Blush	Single	Medium	Summer	5	Bush	Wide	Shrub
R. X Pruhoniciana	c 1920	Moy H	Crimson	Single	Medium	Summer	2	Bush	Tall, wide	Shrub (hips)
Rose Gaujard	1957	HT	Pink/white	Pointed	Large	R very good	1	Bush	Normal	Bedding
Rouletii	1922	Min	Pink	Open	Very small	R average	1	Bush	Small	Pot
Royal Highness	1962	HT	Blush	Pointed	Very large	R average	7	Bush	Upright	Show
Rumba	1958	Flor	Yellow (red)	Full	Medium	R good	4	Bush	Normal	Bedding
Sander's White	1912	Wich H	White	Pompon	Small	Summer	6	Trailer	Normal	Pillar, fence
Scarlet Gem	1961	Min	Scarlet	Neat	Very small	R good	2	Bush	Small	Border, pot
Scharlachglut (Scarlet Fire)	1952	Gall H	Bright red	Single	Large	Summer	3	Bush	Arching	Shrub, fence
Schneezwerg	1912	Rug H	White	Semi-dble	Medium	R good	5	Bush	Vigorous	Shrub
Schoolgirl	1964	Cl HT	Apricot	Pointed	Large	R average	4	Climber	Normal	Wall
Sea Foam	1964	Wich H	White	Full	Small	R average	2	Trailer	Restrained	Weeping Std
Sea Pearl	1964	Flor	Blush (orange)	Pointed	Large	R good	3	Bush	Upright	Bedding
Serratipetala	1912	H China	Red/pink	Frilled	Medium	R average	2	Bush	Short	Interest
Shocking Blue	1974	Flor	Purple	Pointed	Medium	R good	4	Bush	Normal	Shrub
Stacey Sue	1973	Min	Pink	Neat	Very small	R good	3	Bush	Small	Border, pot
Summer Holiday	1969	HT	Vermilion	Open	Large	R good	2	Bush	Normal	Bedding
Temple Bells	1973	Wich H	White	Single	Very small	Summer	3	Trailer	Vigorous	Ground cover
The Garland	1835	Cl Poly	Blush	Semi-dble	Small	Summer	6	Climber	Vigorous	Fence
Topsi	1971	Flor	Scarlet	Semi-dble	Medium	R excellent	2	Bush	Short	Border
Tour de Malakoff	1856	Cent	Mauve	Full	Large	Summer	4	Bush	Wide	Shrub
Toy Clown	1966	Min	White/pink	Neat	Very small	R good	2	Bush	Small	Border, pot
Troika (Royal Dane)	1972	HT	Orange red	Pointed	Large	R good	3	Bush	Normal	Bedding
Tuscany	?	Gallica	Maroon	Semi-dble	Medium	Summer	3	Bush	Upright	Shrub
Tuscany Superb	?	Gallica	Maroon	Open	Medium	Summer	3	Bush	Upright	Shrub
Vanguard	1932	Rug H	Orange pink	Full	Very large	Summer	4	Bush	Tall	Shrub, fence
Vanity	1920	H Musk	Pink	Single	Large	R average	4	Climber	Normal	Fence
Veilchenblau (Violet Blue)	1909	Cl Poly	Lilac	Semi-dble	Small	Summer	4	Climber	Normal	Pillar
Vera Dalton	1961	Flor	Pink	Open	Large	R very good	3	Bush	Normal	Bedding
Virgo	1947	HT	White	Pointed	Large	R good	2	Bush	Restrained	Cutting
Wedding Day	1950	Sinow H	White to pink	Single	Very small	Summer	5	Climber	Normal	Pillar, fence
Whisky Mac	1967	HT	Apricot	Pointed	Large	R average	7	Bush	Restrained	Cutting
White Christmas	1953	HT	White	Pointed	Very large	R good	4	Bush	Normal	Show
White Cockade	1969	Cl Flor	White	Pointed	Medium	R good	3	Climber	Restrained	Wall
Wilhelm (Skyrocket)	1934	H Musk	Red	Semi-dble	Medium	R good	1	Bush	Vigorous	Shrub
William Allen Richardson	1878	Nois	Buff yellow	Quartered	Small	R moderate	4	Climber	Normal	Wall
William Lobb	1855	Moss	Purple	Open	Large	Summer	4	Bush	Vigorous	Shrub
William III	c 1810	Spin H	Purple	Open	Small	Late spring	3	Bush	Short	Border
Williams' Double Yellow	c 1828	Spin H	Yellow	Full	Medium	Late spring	6	Bush	Compact	Border
Woburn Abbey	1962	Flor	Orange	Open	Medium	R average	3	Bush	Upright	Shrub
Yvonne Rabier	1910	Flor	White	Open	Small	R good	5	Bush	Short	Border
Zorina	1965	Flor	Orange	Neat	Medium	R very good	2	Bush	Normal	Cutting (glass)

Abbreviations Used in Class List

Banks	Banksianae	Eglan H	Eglanteria Hybrid	Hug H	Hugonis Hybrid	Poly	Polyantha
Bourb	Bourbon	Filip H	Filipes Hybrid	Kord H	Kordesii Hybrid	Rug H	Rugosa Hybrid
Carol	Carolinae	Flor	Floribunda	Laev H	Laevigata Hybrid	Semp H	Sempervirens Hybrid
Cent	Centifolia	Foet H	Foetida Hybrid	Macro H	Macrophylla Hybrid	Sinow H	Sinowilsonii Hybrid
Cinn	Cinnamomeae	Gall H	Gallica Hybrid	Min	Miniature	Setig H	Setigera Hybrid
Cl Flor	Climbing Floribunda	H China	Hybrid China	Mosch H	Moschata Hybrid	Spin H	Spinosissima Hybrid
Cl HT	Climbing Hybrid Tea	Hesper	Hesperrhodos	Moy H	Moyesii Hybrid	Synstyl	Synstylae
Cl Min	Climbing Miniature	H Musk	Hybrid Musk	Nois	Noisette	Wich H	Wichuraiana Hybrid
Cl Poly	Climbing Polyantha	H Perp	Hybrid Perpetual	Pimp	Pimpinellifoliae		
Cl Tea	Climbing Tea	HT	Hybrid Tea	Platyrh	Platyrhodon		

ROSE GARDENS TO VISIT

We believe at the time of going to press that these gardens are open for public visits; but as conditions and opening times may change from year to year, prospective visitors are advised to check before making their journey.

Austria
Baden bei Wien: Österreichisches Rosarium.

Belgium
Genk: Rozentuin Koningin Astridpark.
Kortrijk: Schloss t'Hooghe, Doornickse Steenweg 281.

Britain
London: Kew Gardens.
London: Queen Mary Rose Garden, Regent's Park.
Romsey: Mottisfont Abbey.
St. Albans: The Royal National Rose Society, Chiswell Green Lane.
Spalding: Springfields.

Denmark
Copenhagen: Valby Park.

France
Lyon: Parc de la Tête d'Or.
Orléans: La Roseraie du Parc Floréal de la Source.
Paris: Parc de Bagatelle.
La Roseraie de l'Haÿ-les-Roses.

Germany. Bundesrepublik Deutschland
Baden-Baden: Kurgarten, Lichtentaler Allee.
Dortmund: Deutsches Rosarium, Kaiserhain 25.
Frankfurt (Main): Palmengarten.
Hamburg: Planten un Blomen.
Insel Mainau: Rosengarten.
Karlsruhe: Rosengarten.
Zweibrücken: Rosengarten.

Germany. Deutsche Demokratische Republik
Sangerhausen: Rosarium Sangerhausen.

Ireland. Eire
Dublin: St. Ann's.

Ireland. Northern Ireland
Belfast: Sir Thomas and Lady Dixon Park.

Italy
Monza: Villa Reale.
Rome: Roseto di Roma.

Netherlands
Amsterdam: Amstelpark.
The Hague: Westbroekpark.

Spain
Madrid: Parque del Oeste.

Switzerland
Geneva: Parc de la Grange.
Neuhausen am Rheinfall: Charlottenfels.

United States
California: Descanso Gardens, La Canada.
Exposition Park Rose Gardens, Los Angeles.
Municipal Rose Garden, San Jose.
Huntington Botanical Gardens, San Marino.
Pageant of Roses Garden, Whittier.
Indiana: Lakeside Rose Garden, Fort Wayne.
Kansas: Rose and Test Garden, Topeka.
Louisiana: American Rose Center, Shreveport.
Missouri: Municipal Rose Garden, Kansas City.
Missouri Botanic Gardens, St. Louis.
Nevada: Idlewild Park, Reno.
New York: Brooklyn Botanic Garden, Brooklyn.
Queens Botanic Garden, Flushing.
Maplewood Park Rose Garden, Rochester.
Ohio: Columbus Park of Roses, Columbus.
Oklahoma: Municipal Rose Garden, Tulsa.
Oregon: International Rose Test Garden, Portland.
Pennsylvania: Hershey Rose Gardens and Arboretum, Hershey.
Longwood Gardens, Kennett Square.
South Carolina: Edisto Gardens, Orangeburg.
Texas: Samuell-Grand Rose Garden, Dallas.
Municipal Rose Garden, Tyler.

NATIONAL ROSE SOCIETIES

Argentina. Rose Society of Argentina, Solis 1348, Hurlingham, Buenos Aires.

Australia. The State Societies in Australia are: The Rose Society of Victoria, 40 Montclair Avenue, Glen Waverley, Melbourne 3150. The Rose Society of South Australia, Inc., 156 Ashbrook Avenue, Trinity Gardens, Adelaide 5068. The Rose Society of New South Wales, 18 Bykool Avenue, Kingsgrove, Sydney 2208. The Queensland Rose Society, Box 1866, GPO Brisbane 4001. The Rose Society of Western Australia, 105 Hensman Street, South Perth 6151. The Rose Society of Tasmania, 656 Sandy Bay Road, Sandy Bay, Hobart 7005.
The National Society is: National Rose Society of Australia, 271 Belmore Road, North Balwyn, Victoria 3104.

Belgium. Société Royale Nationale Les Amis de la Rose, Vrijheidslaan 28, B-9000 Gent.

Bermuda. Bermuda Rose Society, PO Box 162, Paget.

Britain. The Royal National Rose Society, Bone Hill, Chiswell Green Lane, St. Albans, Hertfordshire, AL2 3NR.

Canada. The Canadian Rose Society, 12 Castlegrove Boulevard, Apartment 18, Don Mills, Ontario M3A 1K8.

Czechoslovakia. Rosa Klub, Praha. The Rosa Klub consists of two sister organizations, one in Prague and the other in Brno.

France. La Société Française des Roses, Parc de la Tête-d'Or, 69459 Lyon.

Germany. Verein Deutscher Rosenfreunde, Postfach 1011, 7570 Baden-Baden.

India. The Rose Society of India, A-267 Defence Colony, New Delhi 17.

Israel. The Israel Rose Society, Ganot-Hadar, PO Natania.

Italy. Associazione Italiana Della Rosa, Villa Reale, 20052 Monza.

Japan. The Japan Rose Society, 4-12-6 Todoroki, Setagata-Ku, Tokyo.

Netherlands. De Roos, Prinses Beatrixlaan 100, Waddinxveen.

New Zealand. The National Rose Society of New Zealand, 11 Donald Street, Karori, Wellington 5.

Northern Ireland. The Rose Society of Northern Ireland, 8 McCormick Gardens, Lurgan.

Poland. Polish Rose Society, Browiewskiego 19M7, Warszawa 86.

South Africa. The Rose Society of South Africa, PO Box 65217, Benmore, Transvaal 2010.

Switzerland. Gesellschaft Schweizerischer Rosenfreunde, Haus Engelfried, 8158 Regensberg.

United States. The American Rose Society, PO Box 30000, Shreveport, Louisiana 71130.

The Rose Societies of the world are important repositories of knowledge; but as far as the individual gardener is concerned, they are centers of friendship and of information about roses in his own country.
One can join a local society in town or village, and the national society too; in either case they are composed of people who love roses, and can greatly add to one's interest and enjoyment in growing the "Queen of Flowers."

SELECTED BIBLIOGRAPHY

Allen, E.F. *A Simplified Rose Classification for Gardeners.* Rose Annual, 1973.
— Fungicides and Insecticides for Roses. Rose Annual, 1979.
American Rose Society. *American Rose Annuals.*
— et al. *Modern Roses 7.* McFarland, 1969.
Foster-Melliar, Rev. A. *The Book of the Rose.* Macmillan, 1905.
Harkness, Jack. *Breeding with Hulthemia persica.* Harkness, 1976.
— *Growing Roses.* Studio Vista, 1967.
— *Roses.* Dent, 1978.
Hessayon, D.G., and Wheatcroft, H. *Be Your Own Rose Expert.* Pan-Britannica, 1976.
Hollis, Leonard. *Roses.* Collingridge, 1970.
Hurst, C.C. *Notes on the Origin and Evolution of our Garden Roses.* RHS Journal, 1941.
Jäger, August, *Rosenlexikon.* Zentralantiquariat, DDR, 1970.
Kordes, Wilhelm. *Das Rosenbuch.* Schaper, 1962.
Krussman, Gerd. *Rosen Rosen Rosen.* Parey, 1974.
Le Grice, E.B. *Rose Growing Complete.* Faber, 1965.
— *The Development of Modern Yellow Roses.* Rose Annual, 1972.
Mastalerz, J.W., and Langhans, R.W., eds. *Roses.* Pennsylvania Flower Growers et al., 1969.
National Rose Society of New Zealand. *Rose Annuals.*
— *Roses Cultural Handbook,* 1976.
Paul, William. *The Rose Garden.* Murray, 1848.
Pemberton, Rev. J.H., *Roses, Their History, Development and Cultivation.* Longmans Green, 1908.
Rivers, T. *The Rose Amateur's Guide.* Longman, 1840.
Rose Society of South Africa. *Rose Growing in South Africa,* n.d.
Royal Horticultural Society. *Dictionary of Gardening.* Oxford, 1956.
Royal National Rose Society. *Rose Annuals.*
— *The Cultivation of the Rose,* 1969.
— *Roses, A Selected List of Varieties,* 1976.
Shepherd, Roy E. *History of the Rose.* Macmillan, 1954.
Thomas, Dr. A.S. *Knowing, Growing and Showing Roses.* Macmillan, 1975.
Thomas, G.S. *The Old Shrub Roses.* Dent, 1955.
— *Shrub Roses of Today.* Dent, 1962.
— *Climbing Roses Old and New.* Dent, 1965.
Watts, Martin. *Rose Grower's Cultural Handbook.* Northampton & District Rose Society, 1975.
Young, Norman. *The Complete Rosarian.* Hodder & Stoughton, 1971.

ROSE INDEX

Numbers in italics refer to illustrations.

The rose names used in this book follow the *International Checklist of Roses* compiled by the International Registration Authority for Roses, the American Rose Society, the McFarland Company.

Aimée Vibert, 43
Albéric Barbier, 14, 45, *103*,
  description, 112
Albertine, 45, *45*, 73
Alec's Red, *19*, 43, 118, *163*
  description, 34
Alexander, *18*, 43, 74, 76, 78, 80,
  86, 120
  description, 33
Alexandra, *see* Alexander
Alison Wheatcroft, 68
Allgold, *44*, 44, *52–53*, 70, 76, 80,
  118, 119
  description, 67
Altissimo, 96, 119, *119*
  description, 108
Ama, 69
American Pillar, 14
Amy Robsart, 48, 142
Andrewsii, 47
Angela Rippon, *see* Ocaru
Anne Cocker, 44, *54*,
  description, 67.
Anne Harkness, 44, *54*
  description, 67
Anne of Geierstein, 7, *7*, 48
Arthur Bell, 44, *55*
  description, 68
Austrian Briar, *see* Rosa foetida
Austrian Copper, *see* Rosa foetida
  bicolor
Austrian Yellow, *see* Rosa foetida

Baby Carnaval, *see* Baby Masquerade
Baby Château, 116
Baby Faurax, 45, 68, *98*
  description, 109
Baby Masquerade, 44, *90*
  description 105
Baccara, 117, *117*
Bad Nauheim, *see* National Trust
Ballerina, 45, *45*, 78, *101*, 110
  description, 111
Bantry Bay, 96
  description, 108

Beauté, 35
Belle Amour, 48
Belle de Crécy, 45
Blanc Double de Coubert, 48, *48*
Blanche Moreau, 46
Blessings, *21*, 76
  description, 35
Bloomfield Abundance, 34
Blue Moon, *see* Mainzer Fastnacht
Blush Hip, 48
Blush Noisette, 43
Boule de Neige, 47
Bourbon Queen, 47
Buff Beauty, 44, *89*
  description, 105
Bullata, 46

Camaieux, 45
Canary Bird, *15*, 42, 74, 79, 80,
  130, 138
  description, 142
Captain Thomas, 109
Cardinal de Richelieu, 45
Catherine Seyton, 48
Cécile Brunner, *11, 18–19*, 42, 74,
  105
  description, 34
Celestial, 48, 79, *130*
  description, 141
Céline Forestier, 43
Celsiana, 46, *46*
Champion of the World, 111
Champney's Pink Cluster, 43
Chapeau de Napoléon, 46, *123*
  description, 138
Charles de Mills, 45, *45*
Charlotte Armstrong, 36, 38, 65,
  70, 109
Château de Clos Vougeot, 108
Cherokee Rose, 42
Chicago Peace, *20*, 76
  description, 34
Chinatown, 115, *115*
Chloris, 48
Cinderella, 44, *90*
  description, 105
Circus, 44, *57*
  description, 68
Circus Parade, 68
Cläre Grammerstorf, 68
Climbing Goldilocks, 107
Cocorico, 72
Cœur d'Amour, *see* Red Devil
Columbine, 110
Common Moss, 46, *46*, 138
Compassion, *94*, 120
  description, 107
Complicata, *130*,
  description, 141
Comtesse du Cayla, 42
Conrad F. Meyer, 48
Coral Cluster, *85*
Cornelia, 44, 79, *91*
  description, 106
Cramoisi Supérieur, 42
Crested Moss, *see* Chapeau de
  Napoléon
Crimson China, 44
Crimson Glory, *37*, 69, 108, *114*,
  116

Crimson Shower, 45, 80

Dame de Cœur, 34, 119
Danaë, 44
Danse du Feu, 44, *96*, 109
  description, 109
Darling Flame, *see* Minuetto
Delicata, 48
De Meaux, 46
Desprez à Fleur Jaune, 43
Devoniensis, 43
Diorama, *20*, 116
  description, 35
Doncasterii, 42
Dorothy Perkins, 45, 111
Double White, 47
Dr. A. J. Verhagé, *20, 36*, 43, 67
  description, 34
Dr. W. van Fleet, 45, 111
Dresden Doll, 44, 119
Duc de Guiche, 45
Duchess of Portland, 47
Duftwolke, *22*, 34, *36*, 43, 116
  description, 35

Easter Morning, 44, 119
Eden Rose, 66
Eduardo Toda, 106
Elizabeth Harkness, *22*, 76
  description, 35
Ellen Poulsen, 45
Ellinor Le Grice, 67, 119
Emily Gray, 45
Ena Harkness, 43, *114*, 120
  description, 108
Ena Harkness, Climbing, *95*,
  description, 108
Escapade, 44, *56*, 76, 78, *88*
  description, 68
Etude, 109
Europeana, 44, *56*
  description, 68
Evelyn Fison, *39*, 71
Evening Star, 117
Excelsa, 45

Fabvier, 42
Falkland, 47
Fantin-Latour, *10*, 46, *46*
Fashion, 117, *145*
Fée des Neiges, *see* Schneewittchen
Felicia, 44
Félicité et Perpétue, 14, *100*
  description, 110
Félicité Parmentier, 48
Fellemberg, 42
Fimbriata, 48
First Love, *22–23*, 43, 70, 109,
  117
  description, 36
Floradora, 70
Fortune's Double Yellow, 42
Four Seasons Rose, *see* Quatre
  Saisons
Fragrant Cloud, *see* Duftwolke
Francesca, 44
Franklin Engelmann, 40
Frau Dagmar Hartopp, *see* Fru Dag-
  mar Hastrup
Frau Karl Druschki, 47, 108

Fred Streeter, 42
Frensham, 57, 78
  description, 69
Friedrich Wörlein, 70
Friesia, 59, 76, 116
  description, 70
Fritz Nobis, 48, 74, 79, 132, 133,
  description, 142
Fru Dagmar Hastrup, 48, 74, 80,
  134
  description, 143
Frühlingsgold, 47, 74, 79, 126
  description, 139
Frühlingsmorgen, 41, 47, 115
Frühlingstag, 140

Gallica Complicata
Général Kléber, 46
Général Schablikine, 43
Geranium, 42, 74, 79, 80, 135,
  143
  description, 144
Gertrud Westphal, 69
Gloire de Dijon, 43, 43
Gloire de France, 45
Gloire des Rosomanes, 47
Gloria Dei, see Peace
Gloria Mundi, 45, 116
Golden Chersonese, 15, 42, 74, 79,
  80, 120, 120, 124, 142
  description, 138
Golden Glow, 112
Golden Scepter, 37
Golden Showers, 44, 97
  description, 109
Golden Wave, see Dr. A. J. Verhage
Golden Wings, 47, 74, 78, 79, 80,
  127
  description, 140
Goldfinch, 45
Goldilocks, 67, 117, 119
Grandpa Dickson, 23, 43, 115, 115
  description, 36

Handel, 44, 99
  description, 110
Hanne, 36
Harisonii, 47, 47
Harkaramel, see Anne Harkness
Heidelberg, 110
Henri Martin, 46
Hermosa, 42
Highlight, 40, 67
Hulthemia persica, 14
Hume's Blush Tea-Scented China,
  42

Iceberg, see Schneewittchen
Independence, 66
Irish Gold, see Grandpa Dickson

Janet's Pride, 48
Jersey Beauty, 45
Joanna Hill, 38, 139, 142
John Waterer, 24, 43, 76, 80
  description, 36
Josephine Bruce, 25
  description, 37
Josephine Wheatcroft, see Rosina
Joseph's Coat, 80

Judy Fischer, 44, 119
Julia Mannering, 48, 142
Juno, 39
Just Joey, 24, 43
  description, 36

Karl Herbst, 37, 40
Kathleen Harrop, 47, 137
Kiftsgate, 42, 42
Kim, 72
King of Hearts, 36, 39
King's Ransom, 37
Königin der Rosen, 67, 70
Königin von Danemarck, 41, 48
Kordes' Perfecta, 25, 163
  description, 37
Korona, 108
Korp, see Prominent
Korresia, see Friesia

Lady Godiva, 112
Lady Hillingdon, 43, 43
Lady Penzance, 48, 132, 159
  description, 142
Lady Sylvia, 38
La France, 43
La Giralda, 141
Lamarque, 43
Landora, 26, 78
  description, 37
Laneii, 46
La Ville de Bruxelles, 46
Leda, 46
Leverkusen, 45, 104
  description, 112
Lilli Marlene, 44, 59, 69, 76, 116
  description, 69
Little Flirt, 44, 44
Little White Pet, 11, 110
Lord Penzance, 48
Louise Odier, 47
Lucy Ashton, 48
Lutea, 47
Lydia, 107

Mme Alfred Carrière, 43, 83
Mme A. Meilland, see Peace
Mme Butterfly, 38
Mme Desprez, 138
Mme Ernst Calvat, 47
Mme Eugène Resal, 42
Mme Grégoire Staechelin, 95
  description, 108
Madame Hardy, 46, 121
  description, 137
Mme Isaac Pereire, 47, 47
Mme Laurette Messiny, 42
Mme Legras de St. Germain, 48
Mme Louis la Perrière, 119
Mme Pierre Oger, 47, 122
  description, 137
Mme Roussel, 43
Madge Whipp, 37
Magnifica, 116, 142
Maiden's Blush, 48
Maigold, 128
  description, 140, 140
Mainzer Fastnacht, 27, 116
  description, 38
Manning's Blush, 77

Maréchal Niel, 43
Margaret McGredy, 39
Margaret Merril, 44, 58
  description, 69
Marguerite Hilling, 47, 74, 79,
  128, 141
  description, 140
Marie Louise, 46
Marie Pavié, 45
Marjorie Fair, 45
Marlena, 44, 58, 72
  description, 69
Masquerade, 105, 117, 76
Matangi, 115
Max Graf, see Rosa kordesii
Maxima, 48
May Queen, 45, 102
  description, 111
McGredy's Yellow, 40
Meg Merrilies, 48, 48, 142
Memorial Rose, 45, 112
Mercedes, 70
Merlin, 71
Mermaid, 18, 42
  description, 33
Michèle Meilland, 27, 40, 43, 74,
  76
  description, 38
Mignon, see Cécile Brunner
Minuetto, 44, 117
Mischief, 26, 43, 66, 115
  description, 37
Miss Edith Carell, 116
Miss Lowe's Variety, 42
Mojave, 28, 109
  description, 38
Monthly Rose, 10
Moonlight, 44
Moulin Rouge, 72
Mozart, 45, 78, 101
  description, 111
Mr. Bluebird, 44
Mrs. Anthony Waterer, 48
Mrs. Colville, 47
Mrs. Herbert Stevens, 43
Mrs. John Laing, 47
Mrs. Sam McGredy, 43, 43

National Trust, 28, 43, 74, 76, 78,
  80, 158
  description, 39
Nevada, 47, 79, 129, 140
  description, 141
New Dawn, 39, 45, 74, 79, 102,
  108, 109
  description, 111
New Penny, 44, 92, 119, 119
  description, 106
Niphetos, 43
Nozomi, 120, 120
Nuage Parfumé, 35

Ocaru, 116
Old Blush, 10, 42, 43, 47
Old Pink Moss, see Common Moss
Opa Pötschke, see Precious
  Platinum
Ophelia, 28, 43, 74, 106
Orange Sensation, 116, 116
Orion, 40

Orléans Rose, 116

Papa Meilland, 117
Parkdirektor Riggers, 45, 118
Parks' Yellow Tea-Scented China,
  42, 43
Pascali, 29, 43, 69, 74, 76, 80, 85,
  119, 119
  description, 39
Paul's Scarlet Climber, 14, 45, 109
Pax, 44
Peace, 30, 34, 37, 38, 40, 41, 43,
  45, 65, 80, 113, 114, 161
  description, 39
  history, 39, 113, 117
Peep o'Day, 31
  description, 40
Peer Gynt, 116, 116
Penelope, 44, 78, 90
  description, 106
Peon, 105, 106
Perla de Alcanada, 44
Perla de Montserrat, 107
Perle des Gardins, 43
Perle d'Or, 42, 110
Persian Yellow, 11, 43, 140
Petite de Hollande, 46
Phyllis Bide, 45, 110
Picasso, 115, 115
Piccadilly, 31, 35, 36, 68, 76, 115
  description, 40
Pink Favorite, 30, 43, 74, 78, 117,
  158
Pink Grootendorst, 48
Pink Moss, see Common Moss
Pink Parfait, 40, 44, 60, 68, 71, 76
  description, 70
Pink Perpetue, 44, 98, 120
  description, 109
Pinocchio, 70
Pompon Blanc Parfait, 48
Pompon de Paris, 44, 99
  description, 110
Poulsen's Pink, 140
Pour Toi, 44
Precious Platinum, 32, 43, 115
  description, 40
Premier Amour, see First Love
Président de Sèze, 45
Prima Ballerina, 35, 107, 116, 116
Princess Chichibu, 61
  description, 71
Priscilla Burton, 115
Prominent, 44, 60
  description, 70
Prosperity, 44

Quatre Saisons, 46, 47, 141
Quatre Saisons Blanc Mousseux, 46
Queen Elizabeth, 35, 39, 44, 60,
  74, 78, 80, 109, 117, 158
  description, 70
Queen of Beauty and Fragrance, see
  Souvenir de la Malmaison

Ragged Robin, see Gloire des Roso-
  manes
Ramblers, 77
Ramona, 42

Rapture, 38
Red Ballerina, *see* Ballerina
Red Dandy, 35
Red Devil, *see* Cœur d'Amour, 32, 43, 115
  description, 40
Red Planet, 40, 115
Red Star, *see* Precious Platinum
Reine des Violettes, 47
Reine Victoria, 137
Rise 'n' Shine, 119
Ritter von Barmstede, 45, 74
Robert le Diable, 46
Robin Hood, 45, 71, 111
Rob Roy, 44, 63, 76
  description, 71
Roger Lambelin, 47, 47
Rosa banksiae alba-plena, 42
R. banksiae lutea, 14, 17, 42
  description, 33
R. banksiae lutescens, 42
R. banksiae normalis, 33, 42
R. bracteata, 33, 42
R. canina, 146
R. carolina plena, 42
R. centifolia rubra, 9
R. chinensis mutabilis, 42, 42
R. chinensis semperflorens, 42, 44
R. chinensis viridiflora, 42, 80
R. cinnamomea, 8
R. ecae, 15, 42, 120, 125, 138, 142
  description, 139
R. eglanteria, 7, 7, 48, 142
R. farreri persetosa, 42, 79, 124
  description, 138
R. ferruginea, *see* Rosa rubrifolia
R. filipes, 6, 14, 42
R. flora alba plena, 9
R. foetida, 11, 15, 42, 125, 140
  description, 139
R. foetida bicolor, 42, 126–127, 142
  description, 140
R. gallica, 7, 15, 46
R. gallica officinalis, 45, 112
R. gallica versicolor, 10, 10, 45, 104
  description, 112
R. gigantea, 43
R. glauca, *see* Rosa rubrifolia
R. helenae, 162
R. hugonis, 42
R. Kordesii, 66, 112, 116, 118
R. laevigata, 14, 42, 42
R. lutea, 9, 139
R. macrophylla, 42, 144
R. macrophylla rubricaulis
R. Milesia, 8, 9
R. moschata, 43
R. moyesii, 42, 143, 144
R. multibracteata, 42, 116
R. multiflora, 44, 45, 111
R. Mundi, *see* Rosa gallica versicolor
R. nitida, 42
R. omeiensis, *see* Rosa sericea pteracantha
R. pendulina, 15
R. phoenicia, 46
R. pomifera, 42

R. primula, 42
R. provincialia, 8
R. roxburghii normalis, 15, 42
R. rubiginosa, *see* Rosa eglanteria
R. rubrifolia, 74, 80, 133
  description, 143
R. rugosa, 15, 45
  characteristic, 48
R. rugosa alba, 48, 135, 143, 162
  description, 144
R. sempervirens, 11, 14
R. sericea pteracantha, 15, 42, 131
  description, 142
R. setipoda, 10, 10, 42
R. sinowilsonii, 14
R. spinosissima, 15, 47, 141
R. spinosissima altaica, 47
R. spinosissima hispida, 47, 74, 79, 126, 139, 147
  description, 139
R. stellata mirifica, 42
R. sweginzowii, 42
R. virginiana, 79, 133
  description, 143
R. webbiana, 42
R. wichuraiana, 14, 45, 111, 112
R. willmottiae, 42
R. woodsii fendleri, 42
R. X anemonoides, 42
R. xanthina, 42, 142
R. X cantabrigiensis, 42
R. X damascena trigintipetala, 46
R. X dupontii, 42
R. X francofurtana, 45
R. X hemisphaerica, 11
R. X highdowniensis, 42
R. X macrantha, 141
R. X pruhoniciana, 42, 134
  description, 143
Rose Gaujard, 49
  description, 65
Rosemary Rose, 68
Rosenwunder, 48
Roseraie de l'Haÿ, 48, 79, 136
  description, 144
Rosina, 44, 92
  description, 106
Rote Pharisäer, 111
Rouletii, 44, 106, 107
Royal Dane, *see* Troika
Royal Gold, 94–95
  description, 107
Rudolph Timm, 69, 71
Rugosa alba, *see* Rosa rugosa alba
Ruth Leuwerik, 68

Safrano, 43
Saga, 62
  description, 71
Sander's White, 45
Sarabande, 44, 64, 74, 76, 78, 79
  description, 72
Sarah van Fleet, 48
Scabrosa, 48, 74, 79, 136
  description, 144
Scarlet Fire, *see* Scharlachglut
Scharlachglut, 45

Schneewittchen, 44, 62–63, 74, 76, 80, 116 description, 71
Schneezwerg, 48
Scotch Rose, 15
Semi-plena, 48, 48
Sensation, 66
Serratipetala, 42
Shailer's White Moss, 46
Shirley Hibberd, 112
Shot Silk, 41, 43, 66, 67
Show Girl, 36
Shrubs, 79
Signora, 38, 65
Silver Jubilee, 43, 51, 80, 118, 118, 160
  description, 66
Silver Lining, 40
Sissi, *see* Mainzer Fastnacht
Skyrocket, *see* Wilhelm
Snow Queen, *see* Frau Karl Druschki
Sœur Thérèse, 140
Soleil d'Or, 11, 43
Sonia Meilland, *see* Sweet Promise, 43, 50, 83, 117, 117
  description, 65
Southampton, 44, 64, 74, 76, 78, 80, 120
  description, 72
Southport, 108
Souvenir de la Malmaison, 47, 79, 122, 138
Souvenir de St. Anne's, 47
Spanish Beauty, *see* Mme Grégoire Staechelin
Spanish Sun, 70
Spartan, 37, 117
Spectacular, *see* Danse du Feu
Spong, 46
Stanwell Perpetual, 47, 129
  description, 141
Stargazer, 64
  description, 72
Starina, 44, 93, 117
  description, 107
Sulfur Rose, 19
Sunblest, *see* Landora
Super Star, *see* Tropicana, 33, 51, 116
  description, 66
Surpasse Tout, 45
Susan Ann, *see* Southampton
Sutter's Gold, 51, 76, 80, 117, 117
  description, 65
Sweet Fairy, 93
  description 107
Sweetheart Rose, *see* Cécile Brunner
Sweet Promise, *see* Sonia Meilland

Taifun, 53
  description, 67
Tapis d'Orient, *see* Yesterday
Tawny Gold, 34
Temple Bells, 45
Ténor, 108
The Fairy, 45, 74, 78, 80, 104
  description, 112
The Garland, 45

Tour de Malakoff, 46
Toy Clown, 44
Troika, *see* Royal Dane, 115
Tropicana, *see* Super Star
Tuscany, 45
Tuscany Superb, 45
Typhoon, *see* Taifun

Vanguard, 48
Vanity, 44
Veilchenblau, 109, 172
Violet Blue, *see* Veilchenblau, 45, 109
Violinista Costa, 52
  description, 66
Virgo, 71
Vol de Nuit, 119

Wendy Cussons, 43, 52, 71, 76, 78, 120, 120
  description, 66
White Bath, 46
White Butterfly, 39
White Cockade, 107
White Moss, 46
Wilhelm, 44
William Allen Richardson, 43
William Lobb, 46
William III, 47
Williams' Double Yellow, 47
Will Scarlet, 44, 44

Yellow Banksian, *see* Rosa banksiae lutea
Yellow Cushion, 72
Yellow Sweet Briar, *see* Rosa foetida
Yesterday, 45, 78, 80, 100
  description, 110

Zambra, 65
Zéphirine Drouhin, 47, 122
  description, 137
Zorina, 70

GENERAL INDEX

Numbers in italics refer to illustrations.

Aitchison, Dr. J. E. T., 139
Albas, 8, 48, 141
All-America Rose Selection, 119
Allen, Edward F., 120, *120*, 138
Armstrong Nurseries, 36, 38, 65, 70, 117
Arranging roses, 83–85
Attar of Roses, 46

Banks, John, 33
Banksians, 14, 33, 42, 114
Barbier & Cie, 112
Beds, 76–77
Bees, Ltd., 37
Beluze, Jean, 138
Bennett, Henry, 114, 120
Bentall, J. A., 111, 112
Bizot, Monsieur, 137
Bobbink and Atkins, 139
Boerner, Eugene, 44, 117
Borders, 80
Bourbons, 10, 46, 47, 137–138
Bracteatae, 14
Breeding (roses), 113–120
Budding, 87–88

Cabbage Roses, *see* Centifolias
Camprubi, Carlos, 66
Caninae, 15, 143
Carlton Rose Nurseries, 34
Carolinae, 15, 143
Centifolias, 8, 46, 138
China roses, 8–10
Cinnamomeae, 15, 144
Climbers, 81, 107
Cochet-Cochet, 144
Cocker, Alexander, 34, 66, 67, 71, 118, *118*
Cocker, James, and Sons, 118
Competition, 84–86
Conard-Pyle Company, 34, 39, 68, 106, 112
Cut flowers, 70, 83

Damasks, 8, 46, 48, 137, 141
Delbard, Georges, 108, 119, *119*
Denmark, 143
de Ruiter, Gerrit, 116
de Ruiter, Gijsbert, 35, 68, 116, *116*, 118
de Vink, John, 44, 105, 106
Dickson, Patrick, 36, 40, 114, 115, *115*, 118, 120

Dog Roses, 48
Dot, Pedro, 44, 106, 108, 141
Ducher, Mrs., 34

Ecae Hybrid, 138
Edwards, Gordon, 143
Eglanteria Hybrids (Sweet Briars), 7, *7*, 43, 48, 142
Eurosa, 15
Exhibiting, 84–86

Feeding roses (fertilizer), 160–163
    organic, 161
Floribundas, 44, 70, 115
    climbing, 108–110
    examples of, 67–72
Frank Mason + Son, 40
Fungus ailments, 168

Gallicanae, 15, 112
Gallicas, 8, 45, 46, 141
Gardening, 73–81
    see also Growing roses
Gaujard, Jean, 65
Germain's Nursery, 70, 109
Graveraux, Jules, 144
Green Rose, 42
Gregory, Walter, 35, 66, 109, 120, *120*
Growing roses, 145–171

Harkness, J. L., 33, 35, 40, 67, 68, 69, 71, 72, 107, 110, 120, 141, 144
Harkness, R., and Company, 120
Health care, 164–168
Hedges, 78–79
Henderson, 110
Hesperrhodos, 15
Horvath, Michael, 111
Hybrid Bracteata, 33
Hybrid Chinas, 34, 42
Hybrid Musks, 43, 44, 105–106
Hybrid Perpetuals, 10, 43, 47
Hybrid Teas, 43–45, 47, 107–108
    examples of, 33–40, 65–67
    history of, 10–11, 41
Hybridization, *see* Breeding

Ilgenfritz Nurseries, 66
Illnesses (rose), 164–168
Indicae, 14
Insects, 166–167

Jackson and Perkins, 40, 66, 69, 107, 117, 118
Jacques, A. A., 110
Johnston, Stanley C., 34
Joséphine, Empress, 138, 144

Kordes, Reimer, 67, 69, 70, 71, 116, *116*
Kordes, Wilhelm, 37, 43, 44, 69, 112, *114*, 115, 116, 118, 139, 140, 142
Kordesii Hybrid, 112

Laevigatae, 14
Lambert, Peter, 111

Lammerts, Dr. Walter E., 70, 108, 117
Laperrière, J., 119
Lee, 141
Le Grice, Edward, 44, 67, *118*, 119
Lens, Louis, 39, 119, *119*
Lens, Victor, 119
Lille, Léonard, 109
Lindquist, Robert, 119
Luxembourg Gardens, 137

Macartney Rose, 42
Macrantahs, 141
Mallerin, Charles, 109, 117
Malmaison, 138
Manda, W. A., 111
Manuring, *see* Feeding roses
Mason, Alan, 40
McGredy, Sam, 36, 37, 39, 40, 68, 108, 110, 114, 115, *115*, 118
Meilland, Alain, 65, 117, *117*
Meilland, Francis, 38, 39, 72, 106, *113*, 117, 118
Meilland, Mme Louisette, 107, 117, *117*
Mildew, 168
Miller (breeder), 111
Miniatures, 44, 46
    climbing, 44, 110
    examples, 105–107
Moore, Ralph S., 106, 119, *119*
Morey, Dennison, 107
Mosses, 46
Moyesii Hybrids, 143–144
Musk Rose, 8, 43, 44

Noisette, Philippe, 43
Noisettes, 10, 43
Norman, Albert, 69, 108, *115*, 120

Oger, A., 137
Olesen, Pernille, 115
Onodera, Susumu S., 120, *120*

Paul, Arthur, 33
Paul, William, 38
Pawsey, Roger, 36
Pemberton, Rev. Joseph, 44, 105, 106
Penzance, Lord, 48, 142
Penzance Sweet Briars, 48
Pernet-Ducher, Joseph, 11, 43
Pests (garden), 164–168
Peterson and Dering, 39
Pimpinellifoliae, 15, 138–142
Planting roses, 150–153
    see also Gardening
Platyrhodon, 15
Polyantha Pompons, 111
Polyanthas, 44, 45
    examples of, 109–111
Portland roses, 10
Poulsen, Niels Dines, 44, 114, 115, *115*, 118
Poulsen family, 44, 115
Prior, 44
Propagation, 87–88
Pruhonice, 143
Pruning, 169–171

Ramblers, 45
Redouté, Pierre Joseph, 138
Ridge, Antonia, 39
Rosa (genus), 11–15
Rosaceae family, 12–15
Roses:
    breeding/hybridization of, 113–120
    care and cultivation, 154–159
        (*see also* Growing roses)
    genetic processes, 113
    history of, 7–11
    parts of rose plant, 12–13
Roulet, Colonel, 44
Rugosa Hybrids, 143–144
Rugosas, 48

Scotch roses, 47
Sempervirens Hybrids, 110
Shepherd, Roy, 140
Simplicifoliae, 14
Soil, 146–149
Somerset Rose Nurseries, 111
Spinosissima Hybrids, 139–140
Sweet Briars, *see* Eglanteria Hybrids
Swim, Herbert, 36, 38, 65, 68, 117, *117*
Synstylae, 14

Tantau, Mathias, 35, 37, 38, 66, 105, 115–116, *116*, 118
Teas, 10, 43–45, 47
Tea-scented China Roses, *see* Teas
Thomas Hilling and Company, 140
Thorns, 142

Verbeek, Gijsbert, 34
Vibert, 138
von Abrams, Dr. Gordon, 39, 117

Walsh, M. H., 111
Warriner, William, 117
Watering, 146–147
Weeks, O. L., 119
Wheatcroft, 106
Wichuraiana Hybrids, 45, 111–112
Wild roses, 7
    characteristics, 42
    examples, 138–144
    list of, 42

Yellow roses, development of, 10–11